# Passing Over and Returning

# Passing Over and Returning

## *A Pluralist Theology of Religions*

PAUL O. INGRAM

CASCADE *Books* · Eugene, Oregon

PASSING OVER AND RETURNING
A Pluralist Theology of Religions

Cascade Books
An Imprint of Wipf and Stock Publishers
199 W. 8th Ave., Suite 3
Eugene, OR 97401

www.wipfandstock.com

ISBN 13: 978-1-62032-813-2

*Cataloguing-in-Publication data:*

Ingram, Paul O.

    Passing over and returning : a pluralist theology of religions / Paul O. Ingram.

    xii + 152 pp. ; 23 cm. Includes bibliographical references (p. 143–146) and indexes.

    ISBN 13: 978-1-62032-813-2

    1. Christianity and other religions—Buddhism. 2. Buddhism—Relations—Christianity. 3. Religious pluralism. I. Title.

BR128 B8 I545 2013

For my wife,

Regina Inslee Ingram

# Contents

# Preface

MY FIRST LESSONS IN interdependence came from my father and mother, Gail Owens Ingram and Lucille Wright Ingram. My parents grew up during the Great Depression and entered adulthood during World War II. Like so many of their generation, they understood by experience that they expressed in words said over and over to their three sons, "no one ever makes anything alone." So I want to thank the good people who helped me "make this book."

My first teacher in History of Religions at Chapman University, Ronald M. Huntington was an artist of a teacher who inspired me to rush headlong into the diversity of the world's religions and see what I could find. I have been rushing into religious diversity ever since, a journey for which I shall be ever grateful. Bert C. Williams was my first philosophy instructor—the only philosophy instructor at Chapman during my undergraduate days. He was Boston Personalist who took a working class kid from Santa Monica on a journey into philosophical and theological reflection that is still ongoing. To Professor Williams, too, I owe a debt of gratitude beyond my ability to pay.

The Claremont School of Theology and the Claremont Graduate University embody the pluralism that is ingredient not only in American culture but also the pluralism within Christian tradition in dialogical engagement with non-Christian traditions of faith and practice. Bringing the plurality of the worlds' religions into dialogue with Christian tradition was an intentional act that began with the first president of the Claremont School of Theology, Earnest Cadman Coldwell. One of the leading New Testament scholars of his generation, he brought a diverse faculty to the Claremont School of Theology that placed students in serious dialogue with cultural and religious pluralism. The teachers to whom I am most grateful are: John B. Cobb Jr., who not only introduced me to the process philosophy of his teacher, Charles Hartshorne, but also to Alfred North Whitehead. Cobb is *the* preeminent process theologian in America, perhaps even the world.

Willis W. Fisher and Loren Fisher were my instructors in the Tanak and biblical Hebrew. But more than this, Willis Fisher encouraged me to pursue history of religions and theologically engage the realities of religious pluralism. No one offered me more encouragement and support during my seminary and graduate student days than Willis Fisher. F. Thomas Trotter was dean of the Claremont School of Theology and the first member of the faculty I met. He also taught courses in theology and literature that encouraged me to bring as much creative writing into my own scholarly work as possible. You knew Professor Donald Rhoads was from New England the first time you saw dressed in his brown tweed jacket puffing on an old pipe as he shuffled across campus to his office. He taught philosophical theology and philosophy of religion and encouraged me to carry on my interest in philosophy that began with Bert Williams. Finally, Jane Dempsey Douglas, the first woman to receive a doctorate from the Harvard Divinity School, was also and the first woman to teach at the Claremont School of Theology. Professor Douglas, who is a Presbyterian, taught Church history and knew more about Luther than anyone I have ever met. For all of these excellent teachers I give grateful thanks.

I have been a member of the Society for Buddhist–Christian Studies since its founding. I wish to acknowledge several members of the society living and dead, who have not only encouraged my work even when they disagreed with my conclusions, but who are good friends and colleagues: Sallie B. King; Frederick J. Streng, who died much too early in 1993; Terry C. Muck; John P. Keenan; Wilfred Cantwell Smith (deceased); Roger Corless (deceased), Rita M. Gross; Alice A. Keefe; Paul F. Knitter; Catherine Cornille; John Berthrong; Edward Shirley; Rubin Habito; Tokuyiki Nobuhara; Taitetsu Unno; Mark Unno; Donald K. Swearer; John Moraldo; Donald W. Mitchell; Grace Burford; Paul D. Numrich; Dennis Hirota; Amos Young; David W. Chappell, the founding president of the Society who died suddenly in 2004; and again John B. Cobb Jr.

Finally, several colleagues in the Department of Religion at Pacific Lutheran University, through daily conversation and departmental colloquia, helped me sharpen my ideas: fellow process theologian Marit Trelstad (Systematic Theology and Lutheran Theology); Kathlyn A. Breazeale, also a process theologian who taught feminist and philosophical theology, tragically died of ovarian cancer in October 2012; Robert L. Stivers (Christian Ethics); Douglas E. Oakman (New Testament); Brenda Ihssen (Orthodox Church History); Suzanne Crawford O'Brien (History of Religions, particularly Native American traditions); and Michael Zbraraschuck (another process theologian). I also wish to acknowledge Religion Department colleagues and friends who have moved on to other colleges and universities: Patricia O'Connell Killen, a scholar of American Religious History and currently Vice-President for Academic Affairs at Gonzaga University; Nancy R. Howell, now teaching philosophical theology at St. Paul United Methodist Seminary in Kansas City, Missouri; and Alisha Batten, now teaching New Testament at the University of Toronto.

Finally, I want to thank two professionals at Cascade Books whose able assistance helped me bring *Passing Over and Returning* to publication. Writers need critical readers, and K. C. Hanson is among the best there are. He is editor in chief at Cascade Books, and his sharp editorial suggestions made me a better writer. Christian Admonson created the book's cover, which I think beautifully symbolizes the themes and ideas of this book. Both K. C. and Christian helped me make this book better than the original draft I submitted and I am deeply grateful.

This book is dedicated to my wife, Regina Inslee Ingram. We celebrated our fiftieth wedding anniversary in 2013. We met as students at the Claremont School of Theology in 1962, and I continue to be amazed by her sensitivity, passion for social justice, and support of my work. Gena is theologically trained and spent her professional life as a medical social worker. A social worker, wife, mother, and grandmother, all roles she embraces with zest and intellect, and I am grateful and amazed by how the grace of her life flows into my life, and those of our children, Gail and Robert, our daughter's husband, David Charles Kinner, and our grandson, David Christian Kinner.

Paul O. Ingram
Mukilteo, Washington

1

# Introduction

IT IS COMMON KNOWLEDGE that religious diversity is a fact of life not only in the present, but also in the past. But the mere fact of religious diversity is not identical with "religious pluralism." "Diversity" points to the existence of numerous religious traditions and practices that have grasped human beings, past and present, almost beyond counting. "Religious pluralism" is a theological and/or philosophical construct about the interrelationships and meaning of the empirical facts of religious diversity. Particularly given the exclusivist claims of most Christian theological reflection, religious diversity presents difficult boundary questions for faithful Christians. Furthermore, the theological pluralism ingredient within Christian faith and practice complicates the theological issues.

Of course, all religious traditions that human beings have affirmed are structurally pluralistic. Just how many interpretations of the Incarnation exist in the history of Christianity? Just how many interpretations of the historical Buddha and his teachings have grasped the allegiance of Buddhists in the past twenty-five hundred years? Just how many interpretations of Confucian and Daoist understanding of the Dao or "Way" are there? Just how many ways have Jews wrestled, and still wrestle, with God's "instructions" (*torah*) about how human beings should live in community with God and with one other? Just how many ways have Muslims tried to figure out how to "surrender" (*'islam*) to Allah's will that human beings live in justice and harmony in community with one another and with the environment?

So given the diversity of religious teachings and practices, how is it possible to affirm one's own religious faith tradition and still remain open to the many other religious traditions that human beings have claimed are authentic guides for human living and dying? How is it possible to acknowledge the truth claims of other religious traditions without compromising the truth claims and practices of one's own tradition? Is it possible to adjudicate between different truth claims, for example Christian theism and Buddhist nontheism? Is active engagement with another religious tradition for purposes of conversion to one's own tradition a valid response to "other" religious human beings? Is it even possible to understand religious traditions other than one's own? Should we even try? Or is it possible, as Richard Dawkins argues, that all religions originated as "survival of the fittest" mechanisms whose teachings and practices are merely useful fictions corresponding to nothing objectively real?[1] Are the religions of the world merely illusions? Is it possible that the world's religions are only as culturally valid as humanity's ethnic identities?

In *The Process of Buddhist-Christian Dialogue* and *Theological Reflections at the Boundaries*, I argued that the normative issues of interreligious encounter demand from Christians focused theological reflection in dialogue with the world's religious diversity and the natural sciences. The present book is about my particular dialogue with the world's religions as a Lutheran Christian. While religious diversity is not new, nor are the questions posed by religious diversity new, what *is* new is that more and more Christians are engaged with the world's religions because more and more people are willing to be informed by insights that are found in religious traditions other than their own. This is perhaps particularly true among progressive Christians. The interesting thing is that openness does not necessarily mean rejecting one's own tradition, even though persons sometimes convert to another tradition or maintain their own religious identity while assuming the identity of another tradition.

As one who has taught history of religious his entire professional life, I know from experience that my discipline is incapable of dealing with the normative issues arising from study of the world's religions. I learned this from past masters of history of religions (*Religionswissenschaft*) like Mircea Eliade, Joachim Wach, Joseph Kitagawa, and my own teacher, Floyd H. Ross, during my doctoral studies. But my students taught me a very different lesson. The very act of engaging a religious tradition other then one's own raises important normative questions historians of religions do not usually engage. So unlike many in my academic field, I did not, because I could not, simply say to my students, "You should talk to the theologians in the Religion Department about such questions."

So caught in the rather dated Cartesian epistemologies of history of religions, scholars in this field usually assume that one should study religions

1. Dawkins, *The Blind Watchmaker*.

as "phenomena" that are best approached through the methods of "phenomenology," according to which religious "data" should be studied at an objective arm's length while setting aside all normative issues and boundary questions. But by bracketing off issues of truth, history of religions offers no help in dealing with the conflict between our commitments to a particular faith tradition and our awareness of the multiplicity of religious teachings and practices. Yet at the same time, history of religions is invaluable for the accurate gathering of information about the teachings and practices of the world religions. So as a practicing historian of religion, I sought to expose my students to the wondrous diversity of humanity's religious experience, not whether what religious persons actually do or practice is true or false. History of religions is the best approach for gathering empirical information about religious diversity. The Christian pluralist theology of religions I advocate is grounded in this information.

This is why I have over the years chosen to wear two methodological hats in my work with students and in my publications: that of historian of religions and that of Lutheran theologian, with neither apology to my colleagues in history of religions nor to my colleagues in theology. My particular pluralist theology of religions combines two assumptions. My first assumption acknowledges the existence of boundary questions and the resulting cognitive dissonance such questions engender. A boundary question is a question that arises in a discipline that is incapable of answer by that discipline's methods. For example in the natural sciences, the scientific methods of contemporary cosmologists can tell us that the universe we inhabit originated in an explosive singularity 13.4 billion years ago and that the universe is still expanding from its initial singularity at increasing speed in all directions. But the methods employed by cosmologists cannot tell us *what* caused the Big Bang. Boundary questions also exist in theology, as anyone knows who has tried to resolve the conflict between human freedom and responsibility and God's determination of all things and events in John Calvin's doctrine of double predestination.

Accordingly, my second assumption is that boundary questions generate the experience of cognitive dissonance.[2] The experience of cognitive dissonance has several interdependent features. Physically, it may an impression of inescapable noise or acute disorder, a sensation of alarm, a sense of imbalance, chaos, at times feelings of nausea or anxiety. These forms of

---

2. The following summary of the dynamics of cognitive dissonance follow the scholarship of B. H. Smith; see *Belief and Resistance*; and *Scandalous Knowledge*.

bodily distress occur when one's ingrained, taken-for-granted sense of how things are, will be in the future, or should be is suddenly confronted by something very much at odds with it. Physically, cognitive dissonance may be experienced as a wave of vertigo, for example, at the sight of human disfigurement.

Besides sensory or aesthetic experience, precepts that engender cognitive dissonance can be intellectual, as well as textual. Thus a sense of intolerable wrongness in some politician's description of the issues at stake in an election, or a fellow academic's theoretical description of an issue, can set one's mind on edge and produce a flurry of corrective intellectual activity: letters to the editor, rebuttals, essays, and books. The corrective impulse here is likely to be particularly energetic when one experiences the wrongness as one's responsibility; not, that is, as one's "fault" but as bearing on one's social and professional identity, so that a response seems summoned and obligatory. In all of this, the goal is to end the pain, to get things to feel right, to get back to normal again. Because the traditional universal truth claims of classical Christian theological reflection assert referential epistemological assumptions, Christian encounter with the world's religions has generated much cognitive dissonance in the experiences of faithful Christians.

Here lies the relevance of cognitive dissonance for the practice of theological reflection as dialogical engagement with the world's religions: If what I believe is true, then how can another human being's skepticism of my beliefs be taken seriously? The stability of all beliefs, all worldviews, all religious traditions depend on a stable of explanations for resistance to that belief, worldview, or religious tradition together with a coherent account of how beliefs, worldviews, or religious traditions are formed and validated. This is the classic role of apologetic Christian theology and Buddhism's "philosophy of assimilation," according to which Buddhism incorporated non-Buddhist ideas and practices into itself—even as Buddhism rejected what could not be assimilated—in transmitting itself throughout South and East Asia.[3]

There exist two solutions to this puzzle: (1) the comforting and often automatic conclusion that the other person is a fool; or (2) persons who disagree with me suffer from defects or deficiencies of character and/or intellect: ignorance, delusion, poor training, or captivity to false doctrines. Both solutions reflect "epistemic self-privileging" or "epistemic symmetry,"

3. Matsunaga and Matsunaga, *Foundation of Japanese Buddhism*, vol. 1, chap. 1.

meaning the inclination to assert that what we believe to be true corresponds to reality, meaning "the way things really are," while people who disagree with us have something wrong with them.[4] Such epistemological assertions are "referential" because they assume congruence between statements and/or beliefs and the determinate features of an external reality that are there to be discovered even if no one discovers them.

In contrast to referential epistemologies, a more controversial idea exists, sometimes described as a "hermeneutical circle": our perceptions and descriptions of the things and experience we encounter cannot be independent either of our prior beliefs about those things or of our more general presuppositions and verbal/conceptual practices rooted in communal assumptions about what is true and what is false, which are also interdependent with the neurological structure of the human brain cross-culturally. This is the starting assumption of constructivist epistemologies. Three points differentiate constructivist epistemologies from referential epistemologies.

First, constructivists *do not* characteristically deny *metaphysically* what realists characteristically maintain: that nature is structured in certain ways inherently objective and that those ways are largely in accord with human perceptions. But constructivists deny that such accounts are fully in accord with the metaphysical structures of nature because nature always escapes the methodological boundary limits of all academic disciplines and is, because of the resulting cognitive dissonance, always more than we can know. Human knowledge is always constrained by boundary questions lurking like Chinese "hungry ghosts" in all academic disciplines. So we have partial glimpses, but never complete knowledge in any field of inquiry.

Third, this means that ideas and concepts operate as elements of larger systems or networks of assumptions, beliefs, and discursive practices that are internally related, and, for that reason, fully normative. This is why terms like "planet," "organ," "disease," "race," "gene," or "intelligence"—and similarly, "knowledge." "science," "reason," or "reality"—have meanings not in fixed relations to particular objective referents, but as parts of historically and culturally specific systems of beliefs and/or practices.

Since the 1960s the constructivist views outlined above have been wrongly interpreted—and criticized as implying—an everything-is-valid-relativism, so that anything goes in the practice of science, theology, or any other academic discipline. In point of fact, no constructivist thinker is a

4. See B. H. Smith, *Scandalous Knowledge*, 154–55.

relativist in this sense, even as they presume that knowledge and belief are relative—in the sense of "relational"—to the social, political, economic, theological, philosophical, and historical-cultural contexts of the knower. But what constructivist *do* affirm is the conceptual and empirical inadequacy of prevailing realist or "objectivist" accounts of method, theoretical construction, and truth. Each chapter of this book assumes a constructivist view of human knowing and how knowledge is achieved. Stated differently, to borrow a phrase from Ian G. Barbour, I have appropriated a "critical realist" stance: knowledge about anything we think we know is always an "inference to the best explanation of the evidence available."[5]

For an historian of religion engaged in theological reflection about the world's religions, the practice of critical realism within the context of a constructivist epistemology points to interreligious dialogue with the world's religions, along with dialogue with the natural sciences, as the most important forms of theological reflection for contemporary Christians. Hence, the title of this book: *Passing Over and Returning: A Pluralist Theology of Religions.*

Since this book is a Lutheran Christian historian of religions' theological reflection on religious pluralism, chapter 2, "Can a Lutheran Be A Pluralist Too?" argues that the defining principles of Luther's theology can support a pluralistic theology of religions that avoids the pitfalls of Christian fundamentalism and postmodernism's debilitating relativism. These principles are: *sola scriptura* ("scripture alone"), *extra nos* ("outside ourselves"), "In, With, and Under," "Three Uses of the Law," "Two Realms," "the hidden and revealed God," and *Theologia Crucis,* meaning "Theology of the Cross."

Chapter 3, "A Pluralist Theology of Religions," tries to specify the basic elements of my pluralistic theology through the lens of Whiteheadian process philosophy. My contention is that objections to the pluralist theology of religions, which I take to mean a history of religions research program, can be met by reformulating John Hick's "pluralist hypothesis" through the categories of Whiteheadian process philosophy. Thus the hard core of my research program agrees with Hick's: all religious traditions reflect culturally and historically limited experiences of a reality that transcends them all, and each religious tradition seeks to describe this reality according to their own distinctive cultural and historical experiences. But this reality is incredibly complex, and the teachings and practices of the world's

5. Barbour, *Science and Religion,* 106–10.

religious traditions are *not* identical; they *do not* affirm identical teachings and practices even though they are in reference to the same Sacred reality. Thus each particular tradition expresses a collection of truths intended to be universal, but are not the full truth. Accordingly, the specific religious traditions of the world constitute a series of auxiliary hypotheses intended to be true accounts of reality even as the teachings and practices of the world's religions are often similar, often different, sometimes contradictory, and occasionally complementary in their differences. A negative corollary of my research program is that some teachings and practices of the world's religions *might not* bear ontological correspondence to a Sacred reality that transcends them all.

Chapters 4–8 are a "thought experiments" in which I as a Lutheran Christian apply my pluralist theology of religions through dialogically "passing over" into Hinduism, Buddhism, Chinese religious traditions, Judaism, and Islam followed by a "return" to the home of my Lutheran tradition. In these chapters I specify what I think Christians can appropriate from these traditions as a means of creatively transforming Christian faith and practice. My contention is that one can engage in such an enterprise without assuming non-Christian Ways are either wrong, as in theological exclusivism, or inferior expressions of truths more fully revealed in Christian teaching and practice, as in theological inclusivism. Of course, each religious tradition I engage in these chapters is an incredibly complex pluralist structure of existence, so I do not claim that I have discussed each of these non-Christian Ways fully or with the depth they deserve. Rather I have focused on what each particular religious tradition has taught me up to this point in my life. I do not claim that other Christians might not find other elements of these traditions more illuminating. Nor do I claim that my theological conclusions after "returning" to my Lutheran heritage would be acceptable to the majority of Lutherans or indeed the majority of Christians. Nevertheless, I do think they deserve serious discussion.

The title of chapter 9 is, "If There is Only One God, Why *Are* There So Many Religions?" As a Christian I have learned from what the historical Jesus taught concerning God's nature as love and God's passion for justice as an expression of love that I need to awaken beyond the limited horizon of my own theological perspective, indeed beyond the limits of Christian tradition itself. For the historical Jesus might have been a practicing first-century Jew, but he taught that God doesn't give a damn about an abstraction called "religion," but passionately cares very much about human beings and the rest of creation. God is not confined by human expectations, even Christian expectations. So as much as possible I need to allow non-Christian perspectives to enter into, enrich, and creatively transform my structure of existence as a Lutheran Christian. This is the case because from within the depth's of God's continuing creativity there exists, as Christian mystics like Margarite Porete and John of the Cross experienced, what Shin Buddhists refer to as an "Ocean of Oneness" beyond orthodox and heterodox, a point at which all religious perspectives are embraced and all theological reflection is left unsaid.

But on this side of the "Ocean of Oneness," the reality Christians name God is not the only name to indicate what the Sacred "names." Pluralism is ingredient within the human condition, which means that we cannot "understand" or signify what the words "God," "Allah," "Brahman," "Dao," or "Emptying" fully mean in terns of a single perspective or principle of intelligibility. Hindu, Buddhist, Chinese, Jewish, and Christian names for the Sacred may symbolically point to Sacred, but they never capture the "object" to which they symbolically point. For as mystics in all religious traditions discovered, God, Allah, Brahman, Dao, and Emptying are not "objects" that are reducible to words, concepts, and doctrines.

So if the mystics are correct, all human knowledge is symbolic and to go deeply into any field—physics, say, or art or theology—requires faith in that field's symbols. As we notice that these linguistic constructs are symbols, we learn to translate them, as we go, into our own familiar idioms. But after a while, with growing understanding and faith, we release them. We learn to let them relate on their own terms, subatomic particle to subatomic particle, paint surface to paint surface, theological construct to theological construct, and only then do we begin to make progress. It is in this sense that Anselm of Canterbury was right: faith is the requisite of understanding in all areas of human experience.

2

# Can a Lutheran Be a Pluralist Too?[1]

THE HISTORICAL JESUS IS reported to have said, "Those who find their life will lose it, and those who lose their life for my sake will find it" (Matt 10:39). I suspect this is the way life works, given the perpetual perishing caused by the Second Law of Thermodynamics. But I do not think this is one of God's "commandments" even though it is part of the structure of existence that God continually creates and sustains. It's simply an aspect of the human condition wrapped in the field of space-time. Or paraphrasing the words of Dietrich Bonhoeffer in *The Cost of Discipleship*, "When God calls you, he calls you to your death." But here's the jackpot, according to St. Paul in 1 Corinthians 15: at the moment of death, everyone—all living beings who have lived, are now living, or will live—whether virtuous or not, whether Christian or not, are confronted by the loving gaze of Christ. God deals us a wining hand we can neither earn nor deserve nor predict in advance, which makes theological reflection a wrestling match with God, much like the one Jacob experienced at the River Jabbok (Gen 32:24–31).[2]

The problem is that theological reflection is an attempt to understand what is transcendent in terms of available knowledge of reality, "the way things really are." But a completely transcendent God cannot be meaning-fully conceived or spoken about, and would be utterly superfluous to the universe in general and human experience in particular. A completely transcendent God is a denial of divine immanence, which also simultane-ously destroys human transcendence. So while God is ultimately ineffable mystery, this does not imply that we cannot say *something* about God, even as we cannot say *everything* there is to say. Transcendence and immanence

1. This chapter is an expanded version of a previously published essay titled "Avoid-ing Fundamentalism and Relativism: A Pluralist Lutheran Theology," 330–37.

2. See Ingram, *Wrestling with God*, preface. All biblical references and citations are from the New Revised Standard Version.

for God and for beings created in the image of God are interdependent. Transcendence is God's "primordial nature," as Whitehead phrased it, while God's immanence refers to God's "consequent nature" ingredient in all things and events.[3]

In what follows I shall argue that the defining principles of Luther's theology can support a pluralistic theology of religions that avoids the pitfalls of Christian fundamentalism and postmodernism's debilitating relativism. These themes are: *sola fide, sola scriptura, extra nos,* "In, With, and Under," "Three Uses of the Law," the "Two Realms," "the hidden and revealed God," and *Theologia Crucis,* meaning "Theology of the Cross." But first a brief account of Luther's historical context.[4]

## Some Historical Context

The first thing to note is that the immediate effect of the Lutheran part of the Protestant Reformation was a tremendous sense of liberation—liberation from the moral and theological legalisms of medieval Catholicism, and more personally, from Luther's own self-torturing efforts to overcome his profound sense of unworthiness because of his failure to fulfill God's demands during his tenure as an Augustinian friar. But as an Augustinian friar and university professor, he became one of the most important theology and biblical scholars of his time. It was his biblical scholarship, particularly his translation and exegesis of Romans 1:17, that laid the textual foundations of the Lutheran part of the Protestant Reformation. As Luther described it:

> At last, by the mercy of God, meditating day and night, I gave heed to the context of the words, namely, "In the righteousness of God is revealed, as it is written, 'He who through faith is righteous shall live.'" There I began to understand that the righteousness of God is that by which the righteous lives by a gift of God, namely, by faith. And this is the meaning: the righteousness of God is revealed by the gospel, namely, the passive righteousness with which merciful God justifies us by faith, as it is written, "He who through faith is

---

3. Whitehead, *Process and Reality,* 342–51.

4. See Ingram, *The Process of Buddhist–Christian Dialogue,* chap. 1 for the specific content of my pluralistic theology of religions.

righteous shall live." Here I felt that I was altogether born again and had entered paradise itself through open gates.[5]

Luther's scholarly insights and translations of the Bible gave him a sense of playful freedom. Still, in his later years Luther's more repulsive traits that contradicted this sense of freedom must not be glossed over, for example his rather bloodthirsty harangues during the Peasant's Revolt and his anti-Jewish diatribes because Jews did not follow his originally friendly invitation to convert to his newly reformed Christian community. But Lutheran tradition does not rest on a personality cult. Liberation, joy, and particularly playfulness are Lutheran traits since the very beginning of the Reformation.

But in the sixteenth century, the Lutheran movement had to theologically define itself by a three-fold opposition to: (1) an increasingly hostile Roman Catholic Church, (2) the legalism of the Swiss Reformers that created sharp divisions between the Lutheran and Calvinist streams of the Reformation, and (3) the antinomianism of the "left wing" of the Reformation. Yet as Lutherans made clear their opposition to theological and moral legalism, they did not reject the idea of objective norms for law and morality. Historically, it has not been easy to balance Lutheran themes of liberation, joy, and playfulness. Luther and subsequent Lutheran tradition developed legalisms of their own in a doctrinal orthodoxy that merely paid lip service to the Christian freedom proclaimed by Luther. I suspect this change gained strength because of Luther's associate, Philip Melanchthon (1497–1560), who constructed the systematic theology of *The Augsburg Confession* in order to compete in the intellectual debates with Catholics and the theologians of the Swiss Reformation.

## SOLA FIDE

According to Luther, justification by "faith alone" (*sola fide*) is the sole means for humanity's redemption. It is this teaching that differentiates mainline Protestant tradition from Roman Catholicism, Eastern Orthodoxy, and all Christian fundamentalist movements. "By faith alone" asserts that God's pardon for guilty sinners is granted and received through faith, meaning, "trust" in God's promise of forgiveness and reconciliation revealed in the

---

5. Spitz, trans., *Preface to the Complete Edition of Luther's Latin Writings* (1545) in *Luther's Works*, vol. 36, 337. Subsequent references to *Luther's Works* will be abbreviated *LW*.

life, death, and resurrection of the historical Jesus as the Christ. Faith is *not* assenting intellectually to a series of doctrinal propositions; it is living in conscious and redirected relationship to God in light of the Christ event.

Nevertheless, the temptation to confuse faith with belief in creeds and doctrines is strong because all human beings are, Luther asserted, in the grip of sin and are incapable of pleasing God through belief or ritual acts or ethical behavior, which is exactly what human beings attempt to do. But God, on the basis of the life, death, and resurrection of the historical Jesus as the Christ (*solus Christus*), grants sinners judicial pardon, or "justification," which is received solely through faith, meaning "trust" in God's promises, not belief in creeds or doctrinal propositions, even Lutheran creeds or doctrinal propositions. More specifically, for Luther faith is experienced as a passive reception of Christ and all his benefits, among which benefits are the active and passive righteousness of Jesus Christ. Christ's righteousness, according to the followers of *sola fide*, is imputed or "attributed" by God to sinful human beings, as opposed to the Catholic doctrine of "infused" of "imparted grace" In other words, God's pardon of sinful human beings is not based on anything human beings do or not do, or believe or not believe, but upon Jesus as the Christ and his righteousness alone, which is received by faith alone.

The notion that human beings are redeemed by "faith alone" was not invented by Luther, but "rediscovered" as he translated the New Testament into German while in hiding from his enemies at Wartburg Castle.[6] In Romans 3:28 St. Paul wrote: "For we hold that a person is justified by faith apart from works of the law." Luther was so convinced that he understood Paul's theology that he did not hesitate to add to the original text when he thought Paul's meaning was not absolutely clear. Thus he added the word "alone" to provide clarification of his understanding of Paul's meaning: "We hold a person is justified by faith *alone* apart from works of the law." What St. Paul was writing about in the first century concerned the proper Christian view of Jewish Law. Luther transposed St. Paul's concern to his own sixteenth-century problems with the "law" of medieval Catholicism's sacramental and moral teachings.[7]

But Catholic scholars correctly point out that Luther sneaked in the word "alone." Luther was not a particularly strict constructionist when it

6. Luther translated the Tanak into German with a team of Wittenberg University faculty members as he consulted with Jewish scholars between 1524 and 1535.

7. See Kittelson, *Luther the Reformer*, 87–96.

came to translating the Bible, nor was he a literalist. For him, linguistic accuracy, though important, was not primary. Of course, he tried to translate the Bible into German as accurately as he could while also communicating his theological standpoint. In this, Luther was not alone. All translations seek to balance the quest for literal accuracy with theological accuracy. For Luther, the purpose of translation was to let God's Word speak clearly through the words in the text as he experienced and understood it.[8]

As stated previously, it is important to understand that "faith" does not mean mere assent to doctrinal propositions. "Faith" (*fides*) is "trust" (*fiducia*) in God's saving grace revealed in the life, death, and resurrection of the historical Jesus as the Christ. "Faith alone" is a rejection of the sort of certainty asserted by every sort of fundamentalism. But "faith alone" cannot be equated with debilitating relativism: it is faith or trust in a very objective understanding of reality—the reality of the redemptive power of Christ. This reality is not a subjective phenomenon within human consciousness, but is a reality outside of ourselves (*extrea nos*), indeed, a cosmic reality.

Throughout Christian history, three ways of attempting to establish religious certainty have been popular: (1) certainty based on inerrant scripture, (2) on an infallible church, or (3) on religious experiences like mystical union with Christ or being "born again." The first method is favored by many strands of conservative Protestant tradition, particularly Protestant fundamentalism; the second by a number of churches, particularly the Roman Catholic Church and the Orthodox Churches; and the third by a large number of mystical or quasi-mystical movements ranging from the experiences of Teresa of Avila, John of the Cross, and Margarite Porete to the more mellow "strangely warmed" heart of John Wesley to the wilder "born again" experiences of Pentecostalism. All three forms of certainty have been undermined by contemporary forms of critical thought: biblical fundamentalism by critical biblical scholarship and contemporary science; ecclesiastical fundamentalism by church history and the sociology of religion; and the fundamentalism of experience by neuropsychologists who have made clear the capacity of human beings to delude themselves, since the only thing a religious experience proves is that one is having a religious experience. The interesting point in this regard is that Luther anticipated all three challenges and responded to them accordingly.

---

8. Luther, *On Translating the Bible: An Open Letter* (1530) LW, Vol. 35, 192. Also see Haemig, "Luther on Translating the Bible," 255–62.

## SOLA SCRIPTURA

The phrase sola scriptura is Latin for "scripture alone": the adverb *sola* ("alone" or "solely") is linguistically related to "ground," or "base"; and scriptura means "writings/scripture." For Luther, *sola scriptura* meant that "scripture alone" is the authoritative guide for the practice of authentic Christian faith. For centuries Roman Catholicism has made its traditions equal to the authority of the Bible as the "second leg of revelation." This resulted in many practices that Luther thought were contradictory to the Bible. Some examples are prayers to the saints and to Mary, Mary's immaculate conception, papal authority, indulgences, and five of the seven sacraments.[9] So when the Catholic Church threatened Luther with excommunication, he replied at the Diet of Worms:[10]

> Unless therefore I am convinced by the testimony of Scripture, or by the clearest reasoning, unless I am persuaded by means of the passages I have quoted, and unless they thus render my conscience bound by the Word of God, I cannot and will not retract, for it is unsafe for a Christian to speak against his conscience. Here I stand, I can do no other; may God help me! Amen![11]

The primary Catholic argument against *sola scriptura* is that the Bible does not teach "scripture alone." Furthermore, it was the Church's "tradition" that decided what texts were to be included in the Bible. And in fact, unlike the Qur'an, the Bible nowhere states that it is the only authoritative guide for faith and practice. But Luther responded that while the Bible itself may not explicitly argue for *sola scriptura*, it does not allow for traditions that contradict its message. That is, Luther argued that "scripture alone" is not so much an argument against tradition as it is an argument against unbiblical, extra-biblical and non-biblical doctrines and practices. For him, the point was that individual Christians have the right, in fact the

9. The Council of Trent (1545–1563) defined the seven sacraments as Confirmation, Penance, Eucharist, Baptism, Ordination, Marriage, and Extreme Unction, popularly known as Last Rites. Luther reduced the sacraments to Baptism and the Eucharist because he believed only these two were "instituted by Christ" and contained God's promise of forgiveness.

10. A meeting of the Holy Roman Emperor Charles V's Imperial Diet at Worms in 1521, at which Luther was summoned to defend his theology. Luther first publically committed himself at Worms to the cause of Protestant reform, resulting in formal condemnation of his theology by the Edict of Worms.

11. See Bainton, *Here I Stand*, 143–44; and Kittelson, *Luther the Reformer*, 161–62.

obligation, to guide their faith and practice according to their own reading of Bible, at times placing their conscience as shaped by the Bible against the authority of any ecclesiastical authority, including Lutheran authorities. Yet Luther did not intend his stance on the authority of scripture alone to give support to individualism in its contemporary meaning. His argued that his "stand" was not "by conscience alone." Still, it can be reasonably argued that an unintended consequence of the Lutheran Reformation was a new understanding of individual autonomy in religious and secular matters.

For me, one of the more remarkable features of Luther's notion of "scripture alone" is the freedom with which he interpreted the Bible. He did not like the Epistle of James because he thought it contradicted Paul's teaching of justification by grace through faith alone. As he translated the Bible into German, he seriously considered throwing James out of his translation of the New Testament. He only refrained from doing so because he was reluctant to undertake unnecessarily radical measures. But he still regarded James as less "scripture" than, for example, Romans. Luther's overriding exegetical principle was: Does a biblical text bear witness to Christ, either in anticipation, as in the Tanak, or directly, as in the New Testament.[12]

While this is not a principle to which most contemporary Lutheran or non-Lutheran biblical scholars would subscribe, Luther's approach to the biblical narratives makes the notion of biblical inerrancy incoherent. As a fundamentalist would affirm that the Bible *is* "the word of God," Lutherans affirm Christ is the Word of God through which Christians should figure out the meaning of the words in the Bible. This is an immense difference and is demonstrated by the fact that modern biblical scholarship originated in Germany in mostly Lutheran theological faculties.

## SATIS EST

According to the Augsburg Confession, written by Luther's close friend and colleague, Philip Melanchthon, it is

> enough (*satis est*) for the true unity of the church that there the Gospel is preached harmoniously and that the sacraments are administered in conformity with the divine Word. It is not necessary for the true unity of the Christian church that uniform

12. Although Luther did not like the Epistle of James, he still occasionally preached on this text and often cited it because he believed it taught ethical values Christians should appreciate.

ceremonies, instituted by human beings, be observed everywhere.
As Paul says in Ephesians 4:4–5: "There is one body and one spirit,
just as you were called to the one hope of your calling, one Lord,
one faith, one baptism."[13]

This is an extremely minimalist definition of the unity of the church.
Other than preaching the gospel (the "good news") and the sacraments
(Baptism and Eucharist), which constitute the Gospel in another form,
everything else handed down by tradition is defined as "ceremonies, instituted by human beings." "Tradition" included in Luther's day the ecclesiastical hierarchy and doctrinal edifice of Roman Catholicism. But this did
not mean that ceremonies and institutions had to be uncritically thrown
out. The early Lutheran part of the Reformation was quite conservative
in this regard. But the point was—and still is—they *could* be thrown out,
which makes a church-based institutional fundamentalism extremely difficult. This is so because the church is not the object of Christian faith. The
gospel is the object of faith, which means the church is merely a vehicle by
which Christian faith is facilitated even as the church is itself product of
the Gospel.

Still, the history of the development of Lutheran orthodoxy makes it
clear that *satis est* was used to create new forms of legalism even before
Luther's death. The theological issue was: Who is to decide whether the
gospel is preached in purity, or whether the sacraments are offered "in accordance with the Gospel?" Post-Reformation Lutheran scholars worked
out elaborate and complex answers as they applied Luther's interpretation
of the "marks of the church," meaning the defining traits by which the true
church could be recognized, that was as detailed as Roman Catholic canon
law.[14] Even so, the Augsburg Confession is still available because anyone
tempted to establish doctrinal certainty about the nature of the church can
refer to it and know that one does not have to be a member of a Lutheran
community to be free in one's attitude toward the institutional church and
its ceremonies, or I would add, the faith and practices of non-Christians.

13. Kolb and Wenger, eds., *The Book of Concord*, 42.
14. According to the Nicene Creed, the "marks" or "attributes of the church" are that
it is "one" or a unity, "holy," "catholic," and "apostolic." Each of these marks or attributes
are interpreted quite differently in Lutheran and Catholic theology.

## Extra nos

During Luther's lifetime, a number of movements commonly known as the "left wing of the Reformation" arose. Some of these movements were pacifist and most were either radically more conservative or radically more liberal theologically than Luther. He referred to these movements as *Schwärmer*, meaning "enthusiasts," a term he used to describe people with wild and overly emotional ideas. What many of the "enthusiasts" had in common was reliance on subjective religious experience as the basis of authentic Christian faith. Luther, even though he was influenced by mystical theology during his years as an Augustinian friar, rejected the "enthusiasts" because of their claim to discern the saving work of God outside Word and Sacrament coupled with their over eager support of revolutionary political movements. He rejected all efforts to establish faith on interior subjective experience.

This does not mean that Luther thought of mystical experiences as illusions. He held a fourteenth-century mystical text called the *Thelogia Germanica* or "German Theology" in high regard, and he was positively influenced my Meister Eckhart's mystical theology and perhaps even secondarily through Eckhart, Margarite Porete's *Mirror of Simple Souls*. What he did dismiss was the notion that faith depended on any form of inner experience. In opposition to the "enthusiasts," he used the Latin phrase *extra nos*, meaning "outside ourselves." In other words, we encounter God's grace as an external reality outside ourselves in scripture, the preaching of the gospel, and in the sacraments, not merely or even primarily in the subjective depths of our experience.

The "means of grace" are hard, material facts. Scripture is a book all persons can read; the preacher stands in a pulpit as a living human being; the sacraments are the hard material realities of water, bread, and wine. While discussing the materiality of the Eucharist, Luther once remarked that we can chew the body of Christ with our teeth. Yet in themselves, these "facts" are simple phenomena—a book written by fallible human beings, an unimpressive preacher with little intellect and perhaps a nasty personality, cold water, stale bread, and sour wine. But grace in the form of the Holy Spirit reaches out to human beings so that we can find God's Word incarnated in these everyday phenomenal realties.

So while Lutheran theology tends to induce skepticism about all attempts to attain religious certainty by means of literalist interpretations of the Bible or the absolutism of church authority, it is equally suspicious about the alleged certainties of subjective religious experience. Which means that Lutheran tradition usually takes a rather sober view of the structure of Christian existence: human beings are fallen creatures and the quest for perfection is as futile as it is illusionary. There are no Lutheran saints, but only human beings that are simultaneously "saint and sinner" (*simul iustus et peccator*)—a soberness that makes it extremely difficult to be a fundamentalist, which is not to say that there have not existed fundamentalist Lutherans.

## In, With, and Under

Originally, this phrase expressed Luther's understanding of the Eucharist and is a middle position between Zwingli's understanding of this sacrament as nothing but a memorial ceremony and the Catholic doctrine of transubstantiation. The Lutheran understanding is that Christ is really present in the Eucharist, but it is neither a memorial nor a miraculous event. Christ is present "in with and under" the bread and wine, which remain unchanged as phenomena.

While Luther originally applied "in, with, and under" to the Eucharist, it seems to me that it can be applied equally to scripture, the church, non-Christian religions, indeed even the cosmos. The Bible is the product of human creativity, and as such is full of errors and contradictions, which scholars and ordinary Christians can explore to their heart's content. But "in with, and under" the Bible—and I think other scriptures—lurks the Word of God. The church is an institution, and like all institutions, full of stupidity and intelligence, unethical and ethical behavior, but "in with and under" the church in all its fallibility the gospel is preserved and preached. In the universe we inhabit the forces that generate life seem perfectly balanced in the midst of much natural destruction on Planet Earth and everywhere else in the universe. It is reasonable to conclude that God is "in, with, and under" the processes of nature as well as non-Christian religious traditions, so that when it comes down to it nothing is ever separated from God. Which means the idea of "in, with, and under" makes it impossible to absolutize the Bible, Christian tradition, or a particular Christian denomination. "In with and under" is an anti-fundamentalist concept that offers Christians support for a pluralist theology of religions.

## Three Uses of the Law

Christian freedom as conceived by Luther can be easily transformed into an anarchic relativism in which anything is permissible. Ethically, this takes the form of antinomianism, literally "opposition to law," in which there are no external norms regulating behavior, but only norms that individuals may spontaneously generate. This view was held by many on the left fringes of the Reformation and is still a view commonly held today by many scholars of postmodernism: there are no objective criteria for determining truth or falsehood, there are only different "narratives." Never mind that post modernist theorists have tried and failed to resolve the incoherency of this view. Is their "narrative" merely one among others?

Be that as it may, the Lutheran doctrine of the three uses of the law was intended to protect against this sort of debilitating relativism. "Law," for Luther, meant the moral principles embodied in the Ten Commandments, which he argued has three "uses." First, there is the law's "civil use" (*usus civilis*), the function of which is to maintain basic justice and social order and has no role in the economy of redemption. Second, there is the "convicting use" (*usus elenchticus*), whereby the law convicts human being because we are all sinners who cannot possibly live up to its demands, so that we are dependent on God's forgiveness. Third, there is the "didactic use" (*usus didacticus*): Christians are, by God's grace free of the law even as it continues to serve as a guide to moral behavior.

Personally, I have always felt uneasy about this three-layered understanding. Still, this particular Lutheran doctrine is a corrective to the notion that Christian freedom means the license to do anything one desires. Again, Lutheran theology is a barrier against both fundamentalism and debilitating relativism, which is not to say that there have never existed fundamentalist Lutherans or Lutherans supporting debilitating relativism.

## Two Realms

The search for a nondual position between fundamentalism and debilitating relativism has political importance given the existence of secular and non-Christian forms of fundamentalism now operating throughout the world. Fundamentalism and debilitating relativism create dangerous barriers to any democratic political system. Fundamentalism balkanizes a society into hostile camps unable to live peacefully together, a danger that is particularly great in a democratic society because democracies ideally reject coercion and require compromises of the sort fundamentalists are incapable of making. The question is, can Lutheran theological reflection meaningfully contribute to democracy?

Lutheran tradition makes a sharp distinction between law and gospel. Unlike Roman Catholicism and Protestant movements linked to Calvinism, Lutheran theology has no notion of Christian law, and consequently no notion of a Christian society or state. The distinction between law and gospel also reflects the doctrine of the two realms. There is the realm of gospel, which is where God is engaged in the redemption of the world. Then there is the realm of law, where God demands that human beings maintain elementary standards of justice. Luther believed that these two realms must not be confused because doing so: (1) leads to subversion of the gospel by legalism, or as Luther expressed it, "by works righteousness," and (2) leads to the misguided notion that, in this world, any society could be governed by the principles embodied in the Sermon on the Mount.

So as Luther once said that he would rather be ruled by a just Turk than an unjust Christian, he also urged that Protestant princes should come to the aid of the Holy Roman Emperor, Charles V (1500–1556), who had done everything possible to suppress the Protestant movement, in defense of Europe against the Turkish invasion. Luther did so not because the Turks were Muslims, but because they murdered, raped, and enslaved people whom the Emperor was required to defend. Luther did not call for a crusade. In his theology the gospel never requires defense by the sword, but innocent people often do. He was not a pacifist and would have probably supported contemporary Christian just war theories.

Of course, the doctrine of two realms has been criticized for making persons subservient to anything done by governments. While Luther did not live in a democratic society—none existed in the sixteenth century—he believed that all rulers, repressive or otherwise, must be obeyed since the realm of the law is instituted by God and requires some form of political system to enforce a society's laws. He thought that citizens have no right to revolt against an oppressive ruler unless that ruler tried to force Christians not to follow God's laws. This fact often lead Lutherans to subservience to anything done by government; but contemporary Lutheran theology generally regards this as a distortion of the doctrine of two realms. Governments and Christian institutions are expected to be just. When they are not, they lose their God-instituted legitimacy and Christians are free to withdraw heir allegiance.

Such withdrawal of allegiance was clearly expressed by congregations of the Confessing Church in Germany, who resisted the Nazi takeover of the Protestant churches. Certainly, very few German Lutherans or Catholics supported resistance against the Nazis. But the minority who did, the best known being Dietrich Bonhoeffer, were motivated by a Lutheran understanding of the proper role of the state that focused on the doctrine of the two realms. Bonhoeffer, as well as other Confessing Christians, suffered imprisonment and execution for his resistance.

Accordingly, the doctrine of the two realms does not support political passivity. It is also a strongly anti-utopian doctrine because the New Testament proclaims the kingdom of God that is yet to come, even though it has been initiated by the life, death, and resurrection of the historical Jesus as the Christ. Any attempt to set up the kingdom of God here-and-now is a distortion of the Gospel, whether by violent or nonviolent means. During Luther's lifetime, the "left wing of the Reformation" started a number of movements involved in utopian causes, among them attempts to initiate the Kingdom of God in the city of Münster, which was suppressed by an alliance of Lutherans and Catholics. The doctrine of the two realms is a barrier against movements promising salvation through political action, whether couched in religious or secular terms. The realm of the law is not to be appropriated in an absolute way, but rather in a way guided by prudent reason.

## The "Hidden" and "Revealed God"

Luther's way of reflecting on God's transcendence was the notion of God's hiddenness, which he did not think of as one attribute of God among others. That is, God's hiddenness is not an attribute in the way love and justice are attributes of God. This would mean that "hiddenness" is merely an adjective modifying the word "God," which would only mean that God is invisible. In fact, it was not so much that God cannot be seen that concerned Luther, but that God actually and actively *hides.* God hides in order not to be found where human beings wish to find God, for example in institutional structures, political systems, or in humanity's religions traditions. Furthermore, God hides in order to be found where God *wishes* to be found.

So "to hide" is an activity of God, a verb whose subject is God. This is why Luther thought it is "fearful thing to fall into the hands of the living God" (Heb 10:31). God does not make God's self known unambiguously in acts of transparent significance, always preserving those who trust God from every misfortune while regularly restraining and punishing the actions of transgressing human beings. Neither prayer nor blasphemy is a magical lever that can be used to switch on God's power to demonstrate God's existence. For Luther, God cannot to be put to the test, either by demand for a particular outcome or by challenge to God's authority.

So when God cannot be found it is because God does not want to be found; God quite literally hides from would-be seekers. But in God's hiddeness God also does something to us. God does not benignly rest in a heaven possessing a substance of some spiritual sort ultimately unreachable by human minds, and there waits for us to make some sort of effort at knowing him by analogy or theological speculation. Instead, God hides within the physical realities of the world.

This aspect of Luther's theology was deeply influenced by apophatic (negative) theology. But he was also a cataphatic (positive) theologian in his view that God's hiddenness is God's way of negating the sinner's own self; by hiding, God negates the sinner's own self in order to make it positive in a new way. While Luther was deeply influenced by his study of the mystics and theologians of the negative way, he did not understand mystical negation as a moment in one's use of analogy to "unsay" what cannot rightly be said of an infinite being. Instead, negation is always the act of God applying the cross to all human expectations, which can be seen in an assertion he once made that goes to the heart of philosophical speculation of his day about God's being:

> In his dialogue concerning being, Plato disputes about God and declares that God is nothing and yet is everything. Eck followed Plato, and other theologians also said that the affirmative definition is uncertain but the negative definition is absolute. Nobody has understood this.[15]

No one can know "what" God is or is not or "where" God is or is not by reason of analogy with human experience of the world that is called "natural theology." We can only know God as God reveals God's self, which for Luther is in the life, crucifixion, and resurrection of the historical Jesus. It is this aspect of Luther's theology that undercuts all religious and theological imperialism and thereby offers powerful Christian justification for

15. *LW* 54:34

a pluralistic theology and makes the practice of interreligious dialogue a theological imperative.

A few years ago I assigned a group of students in a senior religious studies seminar to read Pierre Teilhard de Chardin's *The Phenomenon of Man*. During our discussion, one student asked if I believed all human beings, including non-Christians, "will be saved." I responded that I hoped all living things, including human beings, are redeemed by God's loving grace, but I do not know that this is the case because I am not God. The religious practices of non-Christians or atheists are between them and God. No one except God, who hides from all human attempts to control God's actions, can know the answer to this boundary question and therefore no one has the right to engage in religious imperialism. But it *is* reasonable to hope that God's loving grace is freely given to all persons and life forms, past, present, and future. Then another student asked, "Does this apply to conservative Christians, fundamentalists, or atheists?" To which I replied, "yes."

## *THELOLOGIA CRUCIS* VERSUS *THEOLOGIA GLORIAE*

In Luther's time, as well as in the present, a major problem facing contemporary Christian theological reflection involved the issue of power. Until the late nineteenth century, Christianity dominated the cultures of Western Europe, not because Christian tradition is truer than other religious traditions, but because Christianity was culturally and politically more powerful than its rivals. The contemporary postmodern critiques of thinkers like Jean-François Lyotard, Jacques Derrida, and particularly Michel Foucault, assert that all claims to truth, including the claims of theology, are merely secret bids for power.

So the question is: Where does power lie? How are clergy and church leaders to use their power? Such questions reflect the sense that the church has often used theology to legitimate its claims to domination. This style of theological reflection is the defining character of "theologies of glory" (*theologia gloriae*), which generally asserts that: (1) God's ways can be generally understood by human reason, (2) God's favor is experienced in the circumstances of life, in particular, life's successes and victories, (3) God is pleased by sincere human self-effort, and (4) faith, meaning "belief," that the historical Jesus as the Christ is God's ultimate revelatory self-disclosure and is the only means of redemption, meaning Christianity is the only path to "salvation."

Theologies of the Cross (*theologia crucis*) are quite different from theologies of glory. "Theology of the Cross" was first coined by Luther to refer to theological reflection that asserts that the life, death, and resurrection of the historical Jesus are the only sources of knowledge concerning God and how God redeems human beings and the world. Luther first used this term in the Heidelberg Disputation in 1518, but he actually very rarely used it in his subsequent theological writings and preaching. Luther was an Augustinian friar at the time representing his order, and first presented his theses that later came to define the Protestant Reformation. To perhaps oversimplify, in contrast to theologies of glory, theologies of the cross generally assert: (1) God's ways are paradoxical and hidden to human reason, (2) God's grace is manifested in the historical Jesus, particularly in his suffering, death, and resurrection, and (3) God is pleased by the historical Jesus as the Christ, not by ecclesiastical institutions, religious traditions, or theological and missionary exclusivism. Lutheran theologians generally claim that theologies of the cross and theologies of glory are incommensurable because of Luther's teaching that human beings are *simul iustus peccator,* meaning "at once justified and sinner." To experience oneself as fully and completely *peccator*—as sinful and yet fully justified (*iustus*) by God's grace—engenders a sense of humility in relation to other human beings and other religious traditions. Such a person can never claim to be better than others, or that his of her religious practice or tradition is superior to others because he or she remains fully a sinner justified by God's grace.

## CONCLUSION

The themes of Luther's theology that I have summarized certainly do not exhaust the depth of his theological vision. Nor do I claim that the majority of Luther scholars would concur with my conclusions regarding the implication of these themes for interreligious dialogue, or my contention that Lutheran theological reflection can support a robust pluralist theology of religions. Nevertheless, I maintain that a pluralist theology of religions is in consonance with the themes of Luther's theology I have described. A Lutheran can be a pluralist too, and in the twenty-first century, ought to be in dialogue with the world's religions. This is so because the defining themes of Luther's theological vision are a resource upon which Christians may draw to overcome both fundamentalism in its many forms and the debilitating relativism of postmodernism in its many forms.

# 3

# A Pluralist Theology of Religions

ACCORDING TO PHILOSOPHICAL THEOLOGIAN John Hick, the empirical facts of religious diversity raise no serious theological issues. It is only when we focus on what he called "the basic religious conviction" that theological issues are raised for faithful Christians.[1] By "basic religious conviction" Hick meant the conviction that the religious beliefs, practices, and experiences of human beings everywhere at all times and in all places are not illusions because they are in reference to a transcendent reality that he generically called "the Real." Whether such convictions are justifiable is one of the important issues of philosophical theology. But Hick's central point is that all religious persons claim that their beliefs and practices refer to a transcendent reality, named and experienced differently within the context of humanity's collection of religious traditions. Borrowing a phrase from Imre Lakotos, this constitutes the "hard core" of Hick's pluralist hypothesis as well as my particular history of religions research program.[2]

The basic religious conviction usually carries an additional claim: one's particular religious tradition is the most valid response to "the Real" because it corresponds to the "the Real" in ways missing from religious traditions other than one's own. But can such claims—which faithful participants in all traditions assert in their own distinctive ways—ever be validated? Hick thought they could not, and I agree. This is so because the religious experiences of human beings occur within the boundary limits imposed by the plurality of human cultural and historical experience. This means that we can only experience and judge truth claims from the particular historical and cultural contexts through which religious faith and

1. *God Has Many Names*, 88.

2. Lakotos, *Criticism and the Growth of Knowledge*, 91–196. For the specific details of my history of religions research program, see Ingram, *The Process of Buddhist–Christian Dialogue*, 7–28.

practices are lived and judgments made. Thus Hick's conclusion: no one can know "the Real" as such but only as mediated through the filters of history, tradition, and culture.

It is this reading of the empirical facts of religious diversity, Kantian in its epistemological assumptions, that leads Hick to posit the pluralistic hypothesis. If (1) the basic metaphysical core of humanity's religious traditions is the existence of an absolutely transcendent reality (the hard core of Hick's theory of religious pluralism), then (2) all of humanity's religious traditions should be understood, in the words of Lakotos, as "auxiliary hypotheses," meaning "different ways of experiencing, conceiving, and living in relation to an Ultimate Reality that transcends all our visions of it."[3]

Accordingly, different expressions of religious experience that engender different teachings, practices, and images are not necessarily contradictory or competitive in the sense that the truth of one entails the falsehood of the other. In Hick's understanding, all religious traditions reflect encounters with "the Real" within the context of their particular historical and cultural perspectives.

Hick's pluralist hypothesis has been unjustly criticized for establishing the truth of multiple religious traditions by reducing them to a single common element. But, in fact, this is not Hick's claim. He understood perfectly well the diversity of truth claims in the world's religions. A Kantian epistemology might allow one to take such an ahistorical position, but Kiantian as he is, Hick did not draw this conclusion. The "hard core" of his theory is that the religious traditions of humanity embody historical experience of an "ultimate reality," which he called "the Real." His auxiliary hypotheses do not reduce the complexity of the world's religions to a single common element.[4]

Accordingly, my contention is that objections to the pluralist hypothesis, which I understand as a history of religions research program, can be met by reformulating Hick's views through the categories of Whiteheadian process philosophy. Thus the hard core of my research program agrees with Hick's: all religious traditions reflect culturally and historically limited experiences of a reality that transcends them all, and that they all seek to describe this reality according to their own distinctive traditions. But this reality is incredibly complex, and the teachings and practices of the world's religious traditions are *not* identical even though they are in reference to the

3. Hick, *An Interpretation of Religion*, 237.
4. Ingram, *Theological Reflections at the Boundaries*, 33–34.

same Sacred reality. Thus each particular tradition expresses a collection of truths intended to be universal, but are not the full truth. So the specific religious traditions of the world constitute a series of auxiliary hypotheses intended to be true accounts of reality—meaning the way things really are—even as the teachings and practices of the world's religions are often similar, often different, sometimes contradictory, and occasionally complementary in their differences. A negative corollary of my research program is that some teachings and practices of the world's religions might *not* bear ontological correspondence to a Sacred reality that transcends them all.

According to Alfred North Whitehead, creativity is "the category of the ultimate characterizing ultimate matters of fact" according to which "the universe disjunctively becomes the one actual occasion, which is the universe conjunctively." In the process, "the many become one are increased by one."[5] As metaphysically ultimate, all things and events, in Whitehead's language, all "actual occasions of experience" and "societies of actual occasions of experience," at every moment of space-time—past, present, and future—are particular manifestations of this universal creative process, including God, whom Whitehead believed is the chief example of the creative advance.

As the primal example of creativity, what Hick calls "the Real" and I call "the Sacred" is not limited by conventional boundaries, since according to Whitehead, God is ingredient in the becoming of all things and events in the universe but is not exhausted by all things and events. My choice of "the Sacred" to designate the referent of humanity's religious traditions is a reflection of my training in history of religions, particularly as practiced by Mircea Eliade. Although "the Sacred" is certainly open to criticism, "the Sacred" seems to me an appropriate designation pointing to the common referent of humanity religious traditions. Yet I also realize that as neutrally as I try to employ it, "the Sacred" carries Western and perhaps even Christian theistic connotations that may not be fully adequate to the experiences of nontheistic religious persons. Even so, if one is careful, this term can be employed as a generic designation pointing to the common referent of all religious experience, practice, and traditions.

So while I realize that my interpretation of religious pluralism is open to the foundationalist charge that it posits a "common ground" that often creates a debilitating relativism because it explains by explaining away real religious diversity and differences, writers who make this claim often invest

5. Whitehead, *Process and Reality*, 31–32.

themselves in interreligious dialogue. How this dialogue is possible without reference to a sacred reality that transcends all particular religious traditions—however this reality is named—is not often clear. My point is that anyone engaged in interreligious dialogue tacitly acknowledges the existence of a common referent to which the collective religious traditions of humanity point, and it serves no purpose to deny it.[6]

In summary, then, "pluralism" is not another name for "diversity." Diversity names the empirical facts of religious diversity, while pluralism goes beyond mere diversity to hermeneutical engagement with religious diversity. Religious diversity is an observable empirical fact. But noting the mere facts of the existence of neighboring churches, temples, or mosques is merely salad bowl notaton. We can study diversity, celebrate it, or complain about it, but mere diversity is not pluralism. Pluralism is an attitude, a theological orientation, a theoretical construct that seeks to coherently interpret and understand the empirical facts of religious diversity.

Furthermore, pluralism as a theoretical construct is neither an ideology nor a Western neo-liberal scheme nor a debilitating form of relativism. Pluralism is best understood as a theological research program, a dynamic process through which we dialogically engage with one another through our very deepest differences. Which means that pluralism is not mere tolerance of "the other." Although tolerance is a step forward from intolerance, it does not require neighbors to know one another. Tolerance can create a climate of restraint, but not understanding. Furthermore, tolerance does little to overcome the stereotypes and fears that often plague the lives of many religious persons when they encounter the "religious other." Pluralism is a theological-philosophical move beyond tolerance based on exclusivist and inclusivist theologies of religions toward a constructive understanding of what to make of the empirical facts of religious diversity.

Nor does pluralism, as a theoretical construct, lead to debilitating relativism. Pluralist theologies of religions do not displace or eliminate deep religious commitments. Pluralism is the dialogical encounter of commitments. Many critics of pluralist theologies link pluralism with valueless relativism, in which all perspectives are equally compelling and as a result, equally uncompelling. Pluralism, they contend, undermines commitment to one's own particular faith with its own particular language by watering down differences in the interests of universality. I consider such views a

6. For a more complete rejoinder to the criticism of "common ground" notions of religious pluralism, see Ingram, *Wrestling with the Ox*, 172–74.

distortion of theological pluralism because pluralism is engagement with, not abdication of, differences and particularities. While encountering people of other faith traditions may lead to less myopic views of one's own faith, pluralism is not premised on reductive relativism because the focus of pluralist theologies of religions is on significant engagement with real differences.

This means the language of pluralist theologies of religions is dialogue. Vigorous engagement, even argument and disagreement, is essential to a democratic society. Dialogue is also vital to the health of religious faith so that we appropriate our faith not by habit or heritage alone, but by making it our own within the context of conversation with people of other faith traditions. Dialogue is aimed not at achieving mere agreement, but at achieving relationship. Dialogue as the language of pluralism is simultaneously the language of engagement, involvement, or participation. Which means that as a theoretical construct, pluralist theological reflection is never finished, but the ongoing work of each generation.

This is so because the experience of the Sacred, which Christians, Jews, and Muslims name God and Buddhists name the Dharma or often Emptying, and Daoism and Confucianism name the Dao, is pretty much a now you-you-see-it-now-you don't affair. Insights sometimes flash through a text or a conversation or a ritual practice and then dissolve into intellectual and emotional fog. But I have read Krishna's instruction to Arjuna in the *Bhagavad-gita* about the plurality of incarnations of Brahman into an unimaginable plurality of deities, and this has helped me comprehend the possibilities God's incarnation in the historical Jesus as the Christ and, according to the prologue to the Gospel of John, in all things and events in creation. I have read Buddhist Pure Land texts through the eyes of Shinran Shōnin and have experienced with him the "other-powered" grace of Amida Buddha's universal compassion, and this has helped me comprehend the grace of God that Augustine and Luther discovered in St. Paul's Epistles. I have read how Elijah hiding in a cave on Mount Horeb met the back side God in "thundering silence" (1 Kgs 19:11–12), and this has lead me to understand how the One God recited by Mohammed in the Qur'an is closer to a person than a jugular vain; this has clarified for me Christian experience of God's interdependent transcendence and immanence. Such experiences, and others, have often stunned me to silence.

Since most religious conversations are monologues, it is important to be clear about the meaning of dialogue that guides the particular theological reflections in this book. First, interreligious dialogue is a conversation between faithful persons of different religious traditions that is without ulterior motives. Lack of ulterior motives is the most important element of genuine interreligious encounter as well as pluralist theologies of religions. Dialogue is a mutual sharing between two or more persons dwelling in faith traditions different from one's own, while openly and honestly sharing one's own faith perspective. Ulterior motives of any sort, for example converting one's dialogical partner to one's own religious tradition transforms the conversation into a monological debate.

Second, interreligious dialogue requires engagement with the faith and practice traditions of one's dialogical partner. Thereby, our own standpoints are stretched, tested, and challenged by the faith and practices or our dialogical partner.

Third, interreligious dialogue requires critical and empathetic understanding of one's own faith tradition. It's a bit like being in love. As we can recognize another human being's experiences of love because of our own experiences of receiving and giving love, so living at the depths of one's own tradition enables us to apprehend the depths of our dialogical partner's tradition. It is not possible to hear the music of another person's faith apart from hearing the music of our own faith.

Fourth, interreligious dialogue presupposes that truth is relational in structure. It may not be quite correct to say that truth is relative, but our sense of truth is certainly relational. From scientific accounts of the physical processes at play in the universe to social scientific theory to theological explorations of humanity's religious traditions, we can only understand from the perspectives we occupy at the moment we understand anything. This is the constructivist claim underlying my views of interreligious dialogue: we can only apprehend whatever truth is from the particular cultural, religious, social, gender-specific standpoints we inhabit. This is why Carmelite nuns practicing contemplative prayer do not ordinarily experience the Buddha Nature underlying all things and events at every moment of space-time. Nor do Zen Buddhist nuns ordinarily experience union with Christ the Bridegroom as the result of "seated meditation" (*zazen*). Since no one and no religious tradition can enclose the whole of reality within its particular institutional and doctrinal boundaries, dialogue reveals that the faith and practice of other human beings can challenge, stretch, and enliven our particular self-awareness as religious persons. In other words, the purpose of interreligious dialogue is mutual creative transformation.

Finally, the practice of interreligious dialogue requires taking risks. It is not for the intellectually and spiritually timid. Openness to the insights of persons living in the depths of religious traditions other than our own is an "odyssey" which John Dunne described as a process of "passing over and returning"—hence the title of this book.[7] In dialogue, most people pass over into the faith and practices of other human beings, learn and appropriate what they can, and return to the "home" of their original tradition. Most of the time, Christians who pass over into the faith and practices of Buddhists, for example, return to their own Christian self-identity, but an identity different from the Christian self-identity experienced before passing over. In the words of John B. Cobb, they have passed "beyond dialogue."[8] The risk is that one's faith and worldview are transformed in unpredictable ways. Sometimes, persons dialogically passing over into another tradition remain there. Sometimes persons experience dual or even multiple religious identities. Interreligious dialogue is not for persons who easily lose their nerve.

Since this book is written as the theological reflection of a Lutheran historian of religions engaged in dialogue with the world's religions, I need to come clean about another presupposition that underlies this and the remaining chapters of this book. My favorite analogy for describing the practice of Christian theological reflection originates in Luther's reading of the doctrine of the Incarnation. This doctrine holds that the historical Jesus was both human and divine. This paradoxical meeting of the two natures supplies the metaphor by which Christians are taught to understand the many interdependent paradoxes of human experience: flesh and spirit, nature and grace, God and Caesar, faith and reason, justice and mercy. When emphasis is placed on the divine at the expense the human—the fundamentalist error—Jesus becomes an ethical and legal authority remote from our experiences. When Jesus is thought of as merely human—the liberal error—he is nothing more than a social worker.

I supposed one could ask why the incarnational balance of the human and the divine is not so obvious to human beings as to be universally accepted. The truth is that human beings find it difficult to live with paradox. Especially in contemporary Western culture inspired by the Enlightenment and Aristotle's logic of noncontradiction, it seems much easier to seek a resolution in one direction or another, and indeed, making such a choice often seems like the most principled option. But the second-century Buddhist

7. Dunne, *The Way of All the Earth.*
8. Cobb, *Beyond Dialogue*, 47–54.

31

logician, Nagarjuna, whispers a warning to postmodern Christians who have ears to hear: "form is emptiness and emptiness is form," which I interpret to mean that the historical Jesus is divinity in history, divinity in history is the historical Jesus.

While I do not think that divinity in history *only* manifests itself in the historical Jesus, the historical Jesus *is* the focal point of Christian apprehension of God within the rough-and-tumble of history. So one way of imagining the pluralist theology that will operate in the remaining chapters of this book is the wave-practical complementarity in contemporary physics. In certain experimental situations, light can be observed to have either wave-like properties or particle-like properties, depending on how one is observing light photons. There appears to be no line separating wave-like behavior from particle-like behavior. It all depends on what an observer is looking for. Or as Ian Barbour describes Niels Bohr's complemenarity principle, "No sharp line can be drawn between the process of observation and what is observed," because photons exhibit both wave and particle characteristics, but not simultaneously.[9] It all depends on whether the observer is measuring the photon's location or velocity, neither of which as far as anyone knows, can be measured simultaneously. Something similar, I think, is going on in humanity's religious traditions, all of which take place within the boundary constraints of historical and cultural contexts. Meditation, doctrinal reflection, prayer, social engagement, chanting, and communal liturgy are how particular religious communities "observe" the Sacred.

So the primary reasons the historical Jesus sent out disciples two thousand years ago, which faithful Christians should imitate in the present, was not to build the church's membership rolls, although I am always pleased when someone associates with a Christian community because they have heard the music of Christian faith. My guess is that Jesus' disciples were pleased as well when this happened in the early Jesus movement. But for the historical Jesus, the primary reason for "going into the world" was to build the Commonwealth of God. Of course, the full achievement of the Commonwealth of God is something that happens by God's grace, and I take it as given that no one would follow the historical Jesus as the Christ to this end apart from the grace of God's call to do so. I also take it as given that Christians can, and should, dialogically engage non-Christian religious traditions as "ways of saving grace" by which God's love and call for liberating justice are revealed to all persons by means of their own religious

9. Barbour, *Religion and Science*, 67.

traditions. In other words, a pluralistic theology of religions should view non-Christian religious traditions as not only "ways of salvation" but also "ways to the Commonwealth of God."

I need to be clear, however, that I am not espousing a variation of Karl Rahner's "anonymous Christianity," according to which non-Christians living according to virtues Christians can recognize as valid are encountered by the same grace Christians experience mediated through the Catholic Church. Rahner assumed that such non-Christians are really "anonymous Christians" without realizing it. What I *am* proposing is that Christians should think of non-Christian men and women living at the depths of their particular faith traditions as co-workers for the Commonwealth of God, not as anonymous assistants or benighted pagans in need of conversion to one of the institutional church's denominations.

## A PERSONAL POSTSCRIPT

About twenty years ago a student showed up in my office with that gleam in her eyes that says "I want to talk about this." It is at such moments that one's students become "hidden teachers," as Loren Eisley once phrased it, because the energy and focus of their questions force one to reexamine ideas germinating in one's mind over a long academic career.[10] Such moments do not often happen. But when they do, usually after intense emotional and intellectual struggle, questions and insights light up a student's eyes like twin lasers. At such moments you know that your students have grown beyond the need for your instruction because they have begun to connect for themselves the life of the mind with the life of faith. They have entered the path of faith seeking understanding, as St. Anselm phrased it, a path traveled by earnest seekers in all of humanity's religious traditions. They are now, like Jacob at the River Jabbok, wrestlers with God (Gen 32:24–31). During such moments I whisper to myself, "Welcome to the journey, kiddo. But stay frosty. It's going to be a bumpy ride with your hip out of joint."

My student's name was Alyssa. The light in her eyes was the only bright thing on that Pacific Northwest morning. I was watching rain falling hard from slate colored clouds that shrouded the tops of Douglas firs and dimpled pools of water beginning to flood the street that ran in front of my office. Like Herman Melville's Ishmael, I was experiencing a "dark

10. I first described this encounter in Ingram, *Wrestling with God*, 15–17. Also see Eisley, "The Hidden Teacher," 48–66.

November of the soul" because the way I handled Alyssa's question in class earlier that morning satisfied neither of us.

The topic of our class that day was John Hick's pluralist hypothesis and his thesis that Christian theology of religions needs to pass beyond "Ptolomaic" exclusivist and inclusivist perspectives to a "Copernican" paradigm shift toward a pluralist theology of religions.

The light in Alyssa's eyes was sparked by my answers to a series of questions that occurred to her as we discussed Hick's pluralist hypothesis in *An Interpretation of Religion* in conjunction with my views on religious pluralism that she had read in my book, *Wrestling with the Ox*, which was *not* a required text for this particular class assignment.

She was frustrated with both books. "I just don't get it," she said. "If there's a single ultimate reality called God in some religions and something else in other religions, I still don't understand why there are so many *different* religions. Why isn't there just one religion for everyone? Do you really agree with Hick that no two religions are exactly alike even though there are family resemblances? Do you really think that all religions are true for the people who practice them?"

"Yes," I answered. "But that doesn't mean that all religious experiences correspond equally to reality or have equal validity. Karl Marx was half right. Any religion can become an opiate that dulls the mind and emotions. But he was also half wrong. Religious traditions have more often than not been means of creative transformation for the persons who practice them. But there are always historical and cultural issues. Everything has to be critically seen within its own particular context."

"But do you really agree with Hick?"

"Yes, but our conclusions are not identical. There's always more than one way to skin a religious tradition."

"Why?"

Because I'm a monotheist. Monotheism means that there exists one God who creates everything. That includes the world's religions."

My answer came with little reflection, unplanned and spontaneous, blurted like the answer to a Zen koan. Nor did my response have much nuance, and Alyssia knew it as well as I. Yet, somehow it rang true, at least for me, and if I am a good judge of gleams in student's eyes, for her as well. So she showed up in my office to reflect with me about the implications of monotheism for theological reflection about the empirical facts of religious diversity—just as I did fifty years ago when my eyes were it lit up by what my first instructor in history of religions had said about religious diversity. Her newly found koan is still my own. I shall take up this koan again in this book's concluding chapter.

# 4

# On Learning to See

*Hinduism*

## PASSING OVER

THERE IS AN EPISODE in Hindu mythology that tells of a time when the Śiva the Destroyer of Worlds and his consort Pārvatī were sporting in their high Himalayan home when in play Pārvatī covers Śiva's eyes with her hand. The whole universe plunged into darkness, for when Śiva's eyes are covered there is no light anywhere, except the fire in his third eye, which always threatens the destruction of worlds. Hindu deities are all-seeing and are said never to close their eyes. From the near disaster of Śiva's and Pārvatī's play, it is clearly a good thing that they do not. For the wellbeing of the universe depends on the open eyes of the gods.

This chapter is about the importance of seeing in the pluralism of Hindu thought and practice. For not only must the gods keep their eyes open, so must we in order to make contact with them as pointers to Ultimate Reality, which Hindus name "Brahman," perhaps best translated as "Sacred Power." So when Hindus go into a temple their eyes meet the powerful, eternal gaze of a deity as they seek to apprehended the deity as clearly as the deity apprehends them in order to see themselves *and* the deity truly as they are. This is called *darśan* or "seeing." According to the plurality of Hindu teachings and practices, ultimate Reality or Brahman can be seen, that is apprehended, everywhere—if we know how to look. Hinduism is vast collection of ways of seeing Brahman manifested in limited forms called "gods" or even, according to the *Upanishads*, in human beings as Self-expressions (Ātman or "Self") of Brahman.

Of course, "seeing" is a metaphor, the central metaphor underlying all Hindu religious traditions, practices, and philosophical traditions. Sight is one of the human senses having an objective quality about it. When we see something there is no doubt that something is seen. Of course we often make mistakes in interpreting *what* we see. We may misunderstand what we see or we may be experiencing an illusion, or indeed we may occasionally see some thing or event truly for what it is. But in the words of St. Paul, we tend "to see through a glass darkly." But *that* we see *something* when an object captures our vision has an absolute objectivity. So Hindus enter a temple intending to "see" the deities as they are, truly and without delusion, just as the gods see us as we truly are. It's like the experience of seeing or apprehending another person as that person really is, or being seen by another person as we really are, without the pretentions and the socially constructed labels we normally wear to cover up who we really are. Often, the experience is like being knocked over by a feather. So when we see something, its there to be seen even as we often do not know exactly what is seen. The experience of "seeing' is always an interpreted event.

In comparison, the running metaphor of Jewish, Christian, and Islamic traditions of monotheism is "hearing," as in the *shema* in Deuteronomy 6:4: "Hear O Israel, the LORD your God, the LORD is One." *Shema* means "hear," "listen," "pay attention." In Islam, the prophet Mohammed was commanded to "recite" the revelations from God he heard mediated through the voice of the angel Gabriel that constitute the 114 chapters of the *Qur'an* ("The Recitations"). Like seeing, hearing has an objective quality about it. When one hears something, *what* one has heard is there to be heard even as one may misunderstand what one has heard or is deluded in interpreting the meaning what one has heard. Sometimes, persons hear truly, without delusion just as sometimes persons see truly without delusion.

So in Judaism, Christianity, and Islam the focus of religious faith and practice is revelation, which does not imply that the metaphor of seeing is absent from Christian tradition, as exemplified by Greek Orthodox iconography or images sculpted and painted in Christian cathedrals or portrayed in stained glass windows. Nor is the metaphor of hearing absent in the complexity of Hindu tradition. But like seeing, hearing is always an interpreted event, so the rabbis, Christian theologians, and legal scholars of Islam spend their lives trying to figure out the meaning of what is heard in revelation. In the pluralism of Christian tradition, theological reflection is, in the words of Anselm of Canterbury (1033–1109), "faith seeking understanding" of what is or has been heard.

Accordingly, what follows is a descriptive account of the pluralism of the ways of seeing that constitute Hindu teaching, faith, and practice in dialogue with my particular Lutheran Christian faith seeking understanding that is rooted in the pluralism of Christian hearing.

## Deities as Incarnations of Brahman

It is important to understand that the meaning of the word "deity" in Hinduism and the Western monotheistic traditions are not identical. In Sanskrit, *deva* denotes a male deity while *devī* denotes a female deity. Furthermore, most Hindu deities are dual-natured, meaning male and female. Generally speaking, the female deity is the "consort" of the male deity as well as the "power" (*shakti*) of the deity. Most often, it is the feminine side of a deity that is active, either creatively or destructively. For before anything new can be created, the old and worn out must be eliminated. So most Hindu's worship the feminine side of a deity in devotional practice. The masculine side of a deity is mostly passive, although there are exceptions, like Śiva the destroyer of worlds together with his feminine side or consort, called either Kāli or Pārvatī.

Another characteristic of the dual-nature of Hindu deities is that both the male and female sides of a deity are creative and destructive, with female deities portrayed as playing the primary roles in both creative and destructive processes. This reflects a theme found in many pre-modern cultures that still survives in Hindu devotional religion. The natural forces running throughout the universe seem cyclical in nature as they create the balances that keep life alive: the cycles of the season, phases of the moon, cycles of fertility and infertility, cycles of life and death. In fact, natural processes seem to be a system of ever-repeating cycles within cycles. In Hindu mythology, even the universe itself undergoes phases of creation and destruction without end or beginning.

So life itself is a cyclic process that requires living in interdependence with the plurality of cycles that balance natural forces. These cycles are most clearly "seen" in the female side of the species that comprise the life forms of this planet. Life requires a balance between masculine and feminine forces. Human females particularly mirror the cycles of fertility and infertility in their bodies, as well as the pain of creating life and the sorrow of death since child bearing was a more dangerous experience in pre-modern cultures than in most contemporary Euro-American societies. Of course males must make their contribution to the cycles of human sexuality, but once made, they become irrelevant to the creation and preservation of new life. To be sure, men should help women as much as possible in nurturing children, but women can bring forth and nurture life without men's help and often do in most cultures, even now. In other words, feminine power is the energy that brings forth life, nurtures life, and furiously protects new life in all species. Since the nature of god or the gods is a reflection of the cultural experiences of a community, the main deities of pre-modern agriculturally based societies are feminine, with male deities usually, but not always, playing a passive role in human affairs. Contemporary Hindu devotional practices are rooted in this ancient tradition, but with a twist.

The classical text that expresses this "twist" is the *Srimad-Bhagavadgita-Upanishad* ("The Teachings Given Near the Sublime Exalted One"), more popularly known as the *Bhagavid Gita* or "Song of the Blessed One," or simply "The *Gita*." Although it is not "scripture" (*sruti* or "that which is heard") it is perhaps the most revered religious text in Hindu tradition and is also one of the most widely read Hindu religious texts in the West. The *Gita* comprises eighteen chapters of the longest epic poem in world literature called the *Mahābhārata* or "Great Epic Poem." The oldest existing text of the *Gita* is that of Śaṅkara (trad. 788–820), a pre-eminent philosopher and proponent of Advaita Vedanta or "Nondual Vedanta," a monistic interpretation of the *Upanishads*, which are the concluding texts of the Four Vedas ("Wisdom") that constitute the scriptural foundations of Hinduism. However, the oldest written texts of the *Gita* are preceded by a long oral tradition going back at least a thousand years. In fact, the *Gita* is a composite of various systems of Hindu philosophy and practices. Accordingly, it is not quite correct to say that the *Gita* is a systematic treatise. It is more like an anthology of multiple of Hindu traditions.

The context of the *Gita* is a conversation between Lord Krishna and the Pandava prince Arjuna taking place in the middle of a battlefield before the start of a civil war. Responding to Arjuna's confusion and moral dilemma about fighting his own cousins who imposed a tyranny on a disputed empire, Lord Krishna—an incarnation of Vishnu the Preserver who is also an incarnation of Brahman—explains to Arjuna his duties as a warrior and prince as he elaborates on reincarnation, *moksa* or "spiritual release," and Karma Yoga, Jñana Yoga, and Bhakti Yoga.

The *Gita* is also grounded in a cosmology that underlies both the *Upanishads* and *Sāṃkhya* philosophy, the most ancient of the six "orthodox" philosophies (*darśana* or "point of view, " from *darśan*). According to this cosmology, ultimate reality is named Brahman. While absolutely transcendent, Brahman is also absolutely immanent in all things and events. That is, Brahman is incarnated in all things and events as the Self-expression (Ātman) of all things and events. This notion is called "the Great Identity" in the majority of the *Upanishads*, literally "End of Vedas." Or in more slogan-like fashion, "Brahman equals Ātman."

The power of Brahman that is self-expressed in all things and events is called *māyā* ("to limit," to "give definition," sometimes "delusion"). The deities experienced by human beings are finite particular "*māyā*-forms," meaning "limited expressions" of Brahman, collectively called *avatāra* or "descents. In chapter 4, Krishna explains:

> Whenever there is a decline of Dharma, O Bharata, and a rise of Adharma, I incarnate myself. For the protection of the good, for the destruction of the wicked, and for the establishment of Dharma, I incarnate myself in every age.[1]

The *Gīta* teaches that there have been innumerable incarnations of Brahman in human and animal form. These forms are called "avatars." These incarnations are partial, limited expressions of the total reality of Brahman, who transcends all incarnated forms. Another way of thinking about the many incarnations of Brahman is to think of them as partial Self-expressions of Brahman, so that a deity is an Ātman form of Brahman. Such incarnations occur through the power of *māya*; by the power of *māya* Brahman assumes the limited forms human beings imagine out of their needs, desires, and intellect to assume the forms of deity human beings imagine in order to meet human beings where they are so as to lead human beings beyond where they are. In other words, this process of serial incarnations of Brahman is in some ways congruent with what Lutheran Christians call "grace." Or in the words of Arjuna:

> In thy body, O Lord, I behold all the gods and the varied hosts of beings as well—Brahmā the Lord, seated on the lotus throne, and all the sages and celestial beings. I behold thee with numberless arms and bellies, faces and eyes; I behold thee, infinite in form on all sides, but I see not Thy end nor Thy beginning, O lord of the universe, O Form Universal.[2]

1. *Gīta* 4:7, in Radhakrishnan and Moore, *A Sourcebook in Indian Philosophy*, 116.
2. *Gīta* 1:15–16, in ibid., 139.

Unlike Christian notions of God's single incarnation of God's Self in the historical Jesus as the Christ, Hindus believe that an incarnation that happened only once would be of no value because the notion of many incarnations of Brahman stands on an externally operating principle *not* dependent upon a localizable event in past history.

The notion of a plurality of incarnations of Brahman is also given another twist in the *Gītā*. The particular form of Brahman revered by any particular human being is a reflection of that person's *svādharma* or "self-nature," meaning the particular collections of mental, emotional, intellectual, and physical experiences that constitute who that person is at any moment of time. According to the Law of Karma, we create who we are by what we have done in the past, are doing now, and anticipate doing in the future. Our deepest Self (Ātman), which is metaphysically identical with Brahman, carries these acts and experiences as a mixture of forms that cover the Self like a blanket. So the majority of persons rarely see, in the sense of *darśan*, who they really are. So human beings generally "invent" images of gods that are projected onto the universe. In this, the *Gītā* and Freudian psychology agree: out of our needs and desires for security, we create gods and project them onto the external universe. *Unlike* Freud, the *Gītā* declares that Brahman assumes the forms of deity human beings create so that the forms of deity human beings create become real Self-expressions of Brahman. As Krishna explains:

> Whatever may be the form a devotee seeks to worship with faith—
> in that form alone I make his faith unwavering. Possessed of the
> faith, he worships that form and from it attains his desires, which
> are in reality, granted by me alone.[3]

So the "form" (*rūpa*) of a deity is a limited phenomenal expression of an ultimate reality called Brahman that transcends all forms. The form is worshipped because it is accommodated exactly to the mind of a devotee. It may be a divinity of the most ancient Vedic orthodoxy (Agni, Indra, Varuna), or of later Hindu devotional religion: Śiva the Destroyer, Vishnu the Preserver, Brahmā the Creator. Brahman allows each person to go along his or her own way of ignorance, which human beings tend to confuse with knowledge and wisdom. Accordingly, through a partial image of a deity, we can "see" Brahman, but only partially, or again appropriating the words of St. Paul, "through a glass darkly." However, the *Gītā* also warns: "But

---

3. *Gītā* 7:21–22, in ibid., 128.

temporary is the fruit gained by [persons] of small minds. Those worshippers of the gods go to the gods; but my devotees come to Me."[4]

So how *should* we train ourselves to see or apprehend Brahman clearly and without delusion? According to the *Gīta* there are three methods or yogas (" to link" or "yoke together") by which one can train oneself to truly apprehend Brahman: Bhakti Yoga, Karma Yoga, and Jñana Yoga. As noted previously, the *Gīta's* assumptions regarding human nature are rooted in Sāṃkhya philosophy, according to which human beings are an interdependent mixture of three *gunas* or "strands": *tamas guna, rajas guna,* and *sattva guna*. All things and events are constituted by a mixture of these three "strands." But one *guna* predominates over the other two and determines the nature of particular things and events. *Tamas guna* is the principle of inertia, that which resists change. *Rajas guna* is the principle of energy and action, while *sattva guna* is the principle of balance between too much inertia and too much energy. For example, fire or a tornado are primarily *rajas guna* phenomena, but the other two *gunas* are also part of a fire and a tornado's nature. In slow moving life forms like banana slugs or tree sloths, *tamas guna* determines the nature of these life forms, although the other two *gunas* are not absent. Finally, a spring day dominated by a weather system that is neither too hot nor too cold nor too wet is a *sattva guna* system that balances out the extremes of *rajas* and *tamas gunas*.

As applied to human beings, the *Gīta* argues for a theory of human nature based on three "psychological types," to borrow a notion from Carl Jung. *Tamas guna* types of human beings are primarily guided by their emotional responses to things and events whenever making a decision or undertaking an action. Of course such persons possess intellect (*sattva guna*) and the energy to leap into action (*rajas guna*), but such persons are most comfortable when guided by their feeling responses to things and events. That is, things or events that "feel" right primarily guide their decision-making, rather than reason or taking action.

My mother must have been a *tamas guna* psychological type, as are most human beings according to the *Gīta*, the evidence for which can be found in people's responses to the political rhetoric of politicians in a US election cycle. My mother hardly ever made a decision or responded to another human being positively or negatively unless her emotional responses told her what to do. When she had to decide between two or more different arguments on any particular issue, she always made her decisions guided

4. *Gīta* 7:23, in ibid.

by her emotions rather than rational argument; ideas either "felt good" or "bad" to her and she made decisions accordingly. It wasn't that she could not take a rational approach to life's issues. She often did, but she just felt uncomfortable doing so and she lived her guided by her feelings, or as she said her "gut," rather creatively and well. Such persons, according to the *Gīta* should pursue some form of devotional practice or Bhakti Yoga.

As the opposite of *tamas guna* human beings, *sattva guna* types are guided mainly by rational analysis of life's issues. *Sattva guna* types might be illustrated by scholars and academics of all stripes who are mostly guided by reason in making choices. While *tamas guna* types or persons "feel" their way through life's questions and issues, *sattva guna* types try to "think" their way through whatever confronts them. For this category of human beings, the *Gīta* recommends the practice of a meditative form of discipline called Jñana Yoga.

Finally, *rajas guna* types of human beings are guided by action as they confront life's problems. That is, such persons typically act out their way through the issues that confront them with little regard to thinking about solutions in advance or feeling their way through a solution. Such persons are "persons of action" who take charge and do what needs doing quickly without too much intellectual reflection or emotional involvement. According to the *Gīta*, warriors like Arjuna and many politicians are constituted primarily by *rajas guna* and should practice Karma Yoga as the best method for apprehending the connection between their deepest selves and Brahman.

## Bhakti Yoga

Emotional persons should begin with their emotions, the *Gīta* advises, in their search for release (*mokaṣa*) from the cycles of birth and death. Bhakti is a Sanskrit term that signifies "to share," "to be loyal," "to separate." Thus *bhakti* denotes an attitude of devotion to a personal deity that is similar to a number of human-human relationships such as beloved-lover, friend-friend, parent-child, and master-servant. Furthermore most Hindus practice some form of Bhakti Yoga and many Hindus regard Christianity, Judaism, and Islam as Western expressions of Bhakti Yoga. It is probably the case that vast majority of religious practices and attitudes are grounded in some form of devotion toward a deity, so that what Hindus refer to as Bhakti generically names the religious practices and beliefs of most human beings in whatever cultural and historical context.

The goal of Bhakti Yoga is to love God—or one's incarnation of God—totally, without ulterior motives of any sort, that is, with no strings attached. Since love is an emotional focus on an object of love, practitioners of Bhakti Yoga reject all suggestions that the incarnated form of Brahman to which they are devoted is in reality that person's deepest Self. That is, most bhaktas insist on the otherness of God. Because of this sense of God's otherness, the goal of Bhakti devotional practices is not to experience one's deepest Self as Brahman. The goal is to love God only, for no ulterior reasons, so that whatever unity one experiences with God is a psychological or "spiritual unity" (cataphatic) in which awareness of the distinction between self and other remains in tact, not an experience of metaphysical unity in which the distinction between self and other disappears (apophatic) that is the focus of Jñyana Yoga.

But it is one thing to say that we should love God utterly; it is quite another thing to explain how. The method for learning how to express disinterested love of God is constituted by three, interdependent practices: *japam*, "ringing the changes on love," and worship of one's chosen incarnation of Brahman. The goal of these three practices is to love God with no ulterior motives, disinterestedly, with no strings attached, even one's desire for release from the cycles of birth and death.

*Japam* is the practice of repeating the name of God continuously in some form of mantra or ritual formula. For example members of the Society for Krishna Consciousness recite, "Hare Krishna, Hare Krishna, Hare Krishna, Hara Hare; Hare Rama, Hare Rama, Hare Rama Hare Hare," over and over again in their devotional practice.[5] Praying the Rosary or the Jesus Prayer ("Lord Jesus, have mercy on me, a sinner.") repeatedly are examples of Christian mantras. Whatever the task, whatever one is doing, the goal is to keep the name of one's deity at the conscious focal point of one's daily activities so that one's daily activities becomes means of loving and serving God. This aspect of Bhakti Yoga is structurally similar to the Christian idea of "praying without ceasing," so that one's daily actions become prayers to God, a practice that is particularly encouraged in Roman Catholic and Greek Orthodox monastic traditions. Everything one does is to be offered to one's deity as a prayer "with no strings attached."

"Ringing the changes on love" highlights in one's religious practice the fact that love has different shades and nuances depending on the

---

5. Rama is another incarnation of Vishnu and is the hero of the Hindu epic, the *Rāmāyana*.

relationship that is involved with the object of love. Love has degrees of intimacy and all should be experienced in one's love for God. Examples abound. There is the attitude of protected toward the protector, the servant toward the master, the receiver toward the giver. Here one experiences God as a mother, father, lord, or master, so that the devotee's experience of love is expressed through the attitude of gratitude and surrender. This expression of love plays a central role in Jewish, Christian, and Islamic traditions.

A more intimate and equal form of love is that of friendship, also present in Jewish and Christian traditions, but not so much in Islam. Here one approaches God more intimately as an equal, a companion and even a playmate, someone with whom one can argue, as in Judaism, or as expressed in the Christian hymn, "What A Friend We Have in Jesus." Friendship with God is the freedom to argue with God, share feelings, fears, hopes, and anger without fearing the loss of God's friendship.

Finally, love is often expressed erotically, which is the fun of the universe. In this sort of relationship, lovers are so intently focused on one another that all sense of separation vanishes. That is, the duality between self and other disappears, if only for a brief moment, as lover and the beloved become one. The language for such intimacy is the language of sexuality, and in Indian iconography a deity in sexual embrace with his feminine counterpart is a popular representation of this aspect of Bhakti Yoga. Such erotic images and language are also found in Christian mysticism.

Finally, God should be worshipped in the form of one' chosen incarnation. Hinduism generally, and the *Gita* specifically, represents the manifestations of God as innumerable. So devotees are encouraged to attach themselves to one particular image of God that reflects the ideal for that person. But the Bhakta need not shun other incarnations. Often in Hindu community rituals, for example, one hears of devotees of Siva singing songs of praise to Vishnu on a day commemorating Ganeśa, the elephant headed "remover of obstacles." Hindu deities are not jealous deities.

## Karma Yoga

The word *karma* is derived from the Sanskrit *kri*, meaning "to do." In its most basic sense *karma* simply means action and the results of action, while *yoga* translates as "practice" or "discipline." So *karma yoga* literally means "the practice leading to union with Brahman through action." The *Gita* discusses Karma Yoga as a way of acting, thinking and willing according to which one orients oneself toward union with Brahman by undertaking everyday duties and obligations (*dharma*) without consideration of personal self-centered desires, likes, or dislikes, or achieving rewards. Karma yoga is "disinterested action, meaning action without attachment to the fruits of action. Karma yoga is often called "the householder's yoga" because of the *Gīta's* recommendation of this path for those actively engaged with communal and family obligations that make it unfeasible to put in the time required to practice meditative forms of yoga.

Krishna explains to Arjuna that work done without selfish expectations purifies one's mind so that for *rajas guna* individuals like Arjuna it is not necessary to remain in meditative solitude in order to attain *mokṣa*. Karma Yoga, Krishna explains, is "skill in action": "To action alone hast thou a right and never to its fruit; let not the fruits of action be thy motive; neither let there be in thee any attachment to inaction."[6]

Karma Yoga, then, is a technique for doing work skillfully by focusing on the immediacies of what needs to be done apart from any thought of achieving results that gratify one's ego. So one should forget one's self in the midst of acting as one tries to "see" Brahman manifested in one's daily activities and in the objects of one's acting in the world. Thus a sick person, an illiterate person, a person weakened by ignorance, one's wife or husband, one's children and friends—all relationships that demand active engagement—are to be seen as manifestations of Brahman and served accordingly without attachment to achieving results for one's own gratifications. Or retranslated into a more Western idiom, "to achieve salvation requires giving up the desire for salvation." In the words of Swami Vivekananda, who was one of the great teachers of Karma Yoga:

> Look on every man, woman, and anyone as God. You cannot help anyone; you can only serve; serve all the children of the Lord Himself, if you have the privilege. If the Lord grants that you can help any of his children, blessed you are; do not think too much of yourselves. Blessed you are. Do it only as a worship. I should see God in the poor, and it is for my salvation that I go and worship them . . . Bold are my words, and let me repeat that it is the greatest privilege in our life that we are allowed to serve the Lord in all these shapes.[7]

6. *Gīta* 2:47 in Radhakrishnan and Moore, *A Sourcebook in Indian Philosophy*, 110.

7. Swami Vivekananda, *Works*, vol. 3, 246–47; cited in Akhilananda, *Hindu Psychology*, 183–84.

In a video on Hinduism that is part of a series on the world's religions called "The Long Search," the narrator interviewed a physician who was also a monk of the Ramakrishna Mission in Calcutta. The Ramakrishna Mission is a world-wide movement based on the teachings of Śri Ramakrishna (1836–86), an ascetic and mystic born in a Bengali village who claimed that his bhakti practice of devotion to Kali, his practice of Jñana Yoga, as well as his practice of Islamic Sufi mysticism experientially confirmed the truth of the Great Identity. "All paths lead to the same summit" was his summary of his experiences of union between Brahman and Atman as described by most of the *Upanishads.*

By this, Ramakrishna meant that all religious traditions and their particular disciplines are like different routes up a mountain. Persons find themselves on the routes that are best for them, just like all back packers travel the routes that are suitable to their particular physical abilities and wilderness skill levels; not all climbers of Mount Rainier, for example, follow the same route to the summit. But all routes up a mountain converge at the summit, just as all religious paths converge in unity with Brahman.

Inspired by Ramakrishna, this monk devoted his life to medically serving the poor living in the slums of Calcutta. "It's like making an offering to God," he said to the narrator. "When I place garlands of flowers around an image of a deity or pour clarified butter (ghee) on the image, I am using the image of the deity I worship to point me toward Brahman. It's the same every time I offer medicine or do a surgical procedure. My patients are images of Brahman." Or appropriating the words of St. Paul, when we serve the poor we serve the "Christ within us" and them.

To be sure, as anyone who knows me understands, I think inclusivist theologies of religions, like Karl Rahner's or Ramakrishna's, are subtle forms of religious imperialism. But I am not prepared to say that this Ramakrishna monk's motivation for medically serving the poor is based on a delusion.


## Jñana Yoga

A seeker guided primarily by reason and intellect should undertake Jñana Yoga. This form of yoga stresses disciplined meditation whose goal is to know by experience what the *Upanishads* call "the Great Identity," meaning "Brahman equals Ātman." While there is no universal meditative method to accomplish this goal, there seems to be three common elements embodied in the collective disciplines of Jñyana Yoga.

The first is hearing. One must sit at the feet of a teacher or guru to receive guided instruction in the techniques of meditation as well as what to look for during the experience of meditation, particularly how to focus one's mind on a single point (*ekāgrata*) so that one drives from conscious attention everything that diverts concentrated focus from this single point. Once one has achieved proficiency in one-pointed concentration on an external object—for example one's breathing rhythm, an external object or mandala, or rhythmic sounds or mantra—than attention is refocused on one's internal physiological and mental experiences. That is, the yogin become the object of concentration. This is a process by which those subjective experiences that make persons falsely believe that they are separate selves are stripped away. "No, I am not my bodily functions because there's nothing permanent about them. No, I am not my mental, emotional, or physical experiences because there is nothing permanent about these experiences. No, I am not reducible to a collection of social labels—white Anglo-American male, husband, father, Lutheran professor of history of religions"—because there is nothing permanent about these experiences and social labels. By means of this stripping away process one gradually arrives at the core of one's identity, the True Self or Ātman that cannot be stripped away because it is a Self-expression of Brahman. At this point, one realizes, meaning knows by experience rather than intellectual assent to a doctrine, that there is no ontological difference between Ātman and Brahman, between one's deepest Self and Ultimate Reality—or if one prefers, "God."

Finally, various elements of the teachings of the *Gītā* that are a protest against the ritual legalism of the Brahmanic traditions and practices according to which priests (Brahmins) sought to bring the power of Brahman under their control. However, the major themes of the *Gītā* are not new because they probably have their origin in a worldview that goes back to India's Indus Valley civilization. Nevertheless, the *Gītā* unified these traditions in a radically new way.

First, the three ways of achieving spiritual release—Jñana Yoga, Bhakti Yoga, and Karma Yoga—are not mutually exclusive methods of practice. They are intimately interdependent and the three yogas can only be distinguished as a matter of emphasis. That is, the three yogas are so interwoven that the *Gītā* draws no sharp line between them. Certainly, a person whose nature is primarily rational might choose to practice Jñyana Yoga, and individuals actively engaged with the world might pursue some form of Karma

Yoga, while an individual whose life is guided by emotional responses to issues, persons, and ideas might be best suited for some form of Bhakti Yoga.

But the follower of Jñyana cannot experience union with Brahman
without loving devotion (Bhakti) to Brahman, for it is love that overcomes
all dualities between self and other, between self and Brahman. Furthermore, the practice of meditation is difficult work, as any one who has practiced any form of meditation soon learns. Ultimately, before one can achieve
the fruits of any action, which is Karma Yoga, one must renounce the fruits
of actions, even those that are supposed to be induced by meditation.

Likewise, one following the Bhakti path cannot love God completely
and utterly without some form of knowledge of God (Jñyana Yoga) since
love overcomes the duality between the lover and the beloved. And reflecting the love of God in the world with no strings attached, disinterestedly,
is the heart of Karma Yoga. The followers of Bhakti Yoga must experience
Brahman in the midst of daily activities (Jñyana Yoga) guided by devotion
to Brahman or some incarnation of Brahman, which is Bhakti Yoga.

Finally, we must reflect on the central question the *Gīta* tries to answer. If we cannot avoid action, how can we act so that our actions are
wise, meaning corresponding to the realities of the contexts within which
we must take action? The *Gīta*'s answer is basically this: actions based on
ignorance about the nature of the world and what constitutes freedom for
human beings are wrong and bind persons to the world of flux; actions
that reflect knowledge of the world gain freedom for individuals because
they are not compulsive. The freedom that the *Gīta* affirms is freedom from
bondage to ego-centered actions that separate individuals from one another and from Brahman. But more than this, one must pursue spiritual release through the practice of methods and teachings most suitable to one's
nature. We are not all on the same religious path, in other words, nor is it
necessary that we should be. Or in more Christiana theological language,
the *Gīta* asserts an inclusivist theology of religions.

## Returning

My apprenticeship in history of religions began in the 1960–61 academic
year, six-and-a-half years before the Claremont Graduate University granted me journeyman status in the community of scholars and teachers in
my field. I had enrolled in a history of religions course as an elective to
complete my philosophy major. On the very first day of the course, the

instructor, Ronald M. Huntington, introduced me to a tantric Hindu saying that hooked me into pursuing history of religions: *nedeva, devam arcayet,* "By none but a god shall a god be worshipped." The lesson of this ancient text, he said, is about what is now called "religious pluralism": the deity one worships is function of one's mind, which means it is a product of one's age, gender, cultural experiences, and history. Very few Hindus disagree with this tantric saying, and while one cannot argue that Hinduism in general supports a theology of religious pluralism, it is certain the *Gīta*'s inclusivist "all paths lead to the same summit" theology is in full agreement with this tantric saying.

It was through reading the *Bhagavad-gīta* that the Christian doctrine of the Incarnation first began to make sense to me. The essential point of this doctrine is that two thousand years ago human beings encountered God incarnated in a Jewish peasant within the rough and tumble of historical existence, and continue to do so in the present through the Holy Spirit. At least according to Luther, God is "in, with, and under" all things and events in the universe since the beginning of the universe and most particularly in the Incarnation of Jesus as the Christ. God is not only transcendent to every image of God, but God is also immanent within all things and events. Muslims would put it this way: God is closer to us then our jugular veins.

Of course, Luther was not a pluralist theologian, and he certainly was not in dialogue with Judaism or Islam, or for that matter with the sixteenth-century Roman Catholic Church. But part of the biblical foundation of Luther's interpretation of the Incarnation was his reading of the Prologue to the Gospel of John. Read through this lens, the *Gīta*'s teachings about an unlimited number of incarnations of Brahman can be appropriated for clarifying and creatively transforming Christian theological reflection about the incarnation of God in the historical Jesus as the Christ. In John's words:

> In the beginning was the Word, and the Word was with God, and the Word was God. He was in the beginning with God. All things came into being through him, and without him not one thing came into being. What has come into being with him was life, and the light was the light of all people. The light shines in the darkness, and the darkness did not overcome it. (John 1:1–5)

Of course, the distinctive Christian doctrine is that the historical Jesus as the Christ of faith is God's *only* incarnation. The *Gīta*'s incarnational theology is not identical with orthodox Christian incarnational theology. Still,

John's Prologue can be read as declaring that all things and events from the moment of creation onward incarnate the creative Word that is God, like an artist incarnates part of him or her self in the works of art he or she creates. Perhaps the following analogy will clarify what I mean. A painting, like Michelangelo's Last Supper "incarnates" his intentions, technical skill, theology, and aesthetic sensitivities. The painting and Michelangelo are not identical, but they are not separate. They are nondual, so that the Last Supper points to not only Michelangelo's artistic skills and intentions, but also to his particular Catholic understanding of Christ. Christ as God's incarnation does not exhaust the reality of God, just as the Last Supper did not exhaust Michelangelo's artistic creativity. In this sense, his painting is an icon pointing beyond itself to his understanding of God.

In a similar, but not identical way, Hindu *avatars* as limited incarnated forms of Brahman point to Brahman without exhausting Brahman. According to John's Prologue everything and event incarnates God's ongoing creativity since the very beginning. Every thing and event, past, present or future is an incarnation of the Word. Or in the language of Whiteheadian process theology, God's creative "initial aim" that all things and events achieve the fullest "satisfaction" of which they are capable is incarnate in all things and events since the very beginning The difference between the historical Jesus and us is that he fully submitted his "subjective aim" for himself to God's initial aim for Jesus and by doing so became the Christ. But God's initial aim is incarnated in all things and events without exception.

Among other things, if I am reading John's Prologue adequately, this means that all things and events are interdependent from the very beginning. Nothing is completely separate from anything else. Seen from this perspective, everything and anything can serve as an icon, an *avatar* pointing to, but not fully capturing, the reality of God. God is always present within us and beyond us because God is present within every thing and event in the universe and well as transcendent to every thing and event in the universe.

The problem is learning how to see transcendence incarnated in immanence, clearly, without distortion. The practice of *Darśan* means using images of God as symbolic pointers to apprehend the full reality of Brahman. The images are not the full reality of God, even as Paul Tillich would say, they "participate" in a Sacred Reality to which they point. Similarly, Christian notions, images, and theological concepts of God are symbolic pointers to a Sacred Reality that transcends all notions images, and theological constructions. For example, the meaning of "God" for a five-year old in pre-school is quite different than the meaning of "God" for a persons at the end of their life span or to someone experiencing great suffering or to an atheist like Richard Dawkins. God cannot be conceived or experienced apart from images, but cling to an image, confuse the symbolic pointer for the reality to which it points, one only has the pointer. This is the error of fundamentalism in whatever religious or secular dress it wears and is what Islam calls "idolatry" (*shirk*). We can only apprehend God through the lenses of a symbolic pointer, but we should not confuse the symbolic pointer for the reality to which it points.

Thus the collective traditions of Christian theological reflection and practice, which perhaps more than any other religious tradition has a tendency to make sharply exclusivist theological claims, has much to learn from the *Gīta*. The internal history of Christianity is a record of orthodoxy violently oppressing Christians and non-Christians in the name of Christ. Of all he world's religious traditions, Christianity has the bloodiest history. Furthermore, the exclusivist theological confusion of doctrines *about* God *for* God continues in contemporary Christian fundamentalism and much Evangelical theology. Of course, there have always been protests against this violent side of Christian tradition within Christian tradition itself. My point is that Christians can appropriate the *Gīta*'s notion that the deity we revere is a symptom of who we are as an antidote to the violent tendencies of Christianity's traditional exclusivist theological claims.

To illustrate, let me conclude this chapter with description of an encounter I had as a seminary student with a woman and her daughter passing out a religious pamphlets door-to-door. I was enrolled in a seminar on the eighth- and seventh-century biblical prophets. One late morning as I was struggling with the Hebrew text of the first chapter of Amos, the poem against the kingdoms surrounding Israel and Judah, I was interrupted by a loud knock at my front door. When I opened the door I was greeted by a middle-aged woman and her daughter holding a large number of religious pamphlets that read, "Have you been born again?"

As the woman offered me a pamphlet, I said, "No thanks. I'm rather busy at the moment and there isn't enough time in the world to read all the religious pamphlets floating around."

"But don't you want to be saved?"

"I'm a Lutheran. People are saved, whatever this means, by faith through grace alone, even if they're not Lutheran. We are not saved by what we believe or by how many times we've been reborn or by how many religious pamphlets we read."

"But don't you believe in he Bible?" she asked.

"Not only do I believe in the Bible, I've seen it," I said rather sarcastically, hoping she would just go away so I could get back to writing my paper.

But she didn't go away but instead asked if she and her daughter could come in so we could discuss the Bible.

So I invited her in, opened my Greek New Testament and Hebrew Tanak on the coffee table and said, "Ok, where do you want to start?" And with that, they left as they said, "We'll pray for you."

I finished my paper late that afternoon, but even as I did a question began to haunt me. What motivates men and women to knock on the doors of strangers passing out religious pamphlets as a means of convincing people that they need their particular experiences and belief systems in order to be "saved"? Knocking on the doors of strangers selling particular forms of religious experience or ideas is not a safe occupation. And yet the pamphlets keep appearing and the knock on the door by religious enthusiasts continues almost unabated. Why do persons undertake such activities when they know that nine times out of ten they will experience some form of verbal abuse or sarcastic derision?

Then I remembered the *Gītā*'s description of the many incarnations of God. Maybe at a bad time this woman and her daughter were motivated by a fundamentalist preacher's sermon about being "born again," and had in fact experienced a new birth. Perhaps this woman was converted to her form of Christian faith because a community helped her overcome a dependency on drugs or alcohol. Perhaps her faith gave her the strength to face a serious tragedy or perhaps an abusive husband. I have no way of knowing. But this woman would not be knocking on the doors of strangers seeking converts to her particular Christian community unless something marvelous had happened to her that glued her life together in a wonderful and perhaps unanticipated way. I am not prepared to say that her experiences are delusions. But delusion *does* occur when we universalize our *particular* religious experiences as normative for *all* human beings. This is the meaning of *māyā*, "delusion," which is the universal tendency to think that the experiences of God we might have capture the total reality of what God is or is not. Or to paraphrase Luther, we should never reduce God to human experiences or images or theological systems of doctrine.

5

# On Learning not to Cling

*Buddhism*

## PASSING OVER

WHAT IS GENERALLY REFERRED to as "Buddhism" is a complex collection of traditions that have evolved for over twenty-five hundred years centered on the life, teachings, and death of an itinerant Indian teacher named Siddhartha Gautama. Likewise, what is generally referred to as "Christianity" is a complex collection of traditions that have evolved for two thousand years centered on the life, teachings, and death of a first-century peasant named Jesus of Nazareth. Yet I must confess at the outset of this chapter that much Buddhist reflection on the Buddha, "the Awakened One," and much Christian reflection on the historical Jesus as the Christ seems to me rather incoherent. I often experience immense cognitive dissonance because I am not always clear about what Buddhists and Christians in dialogue are talking about when they talk about the historical Buddha or the historical Jesus. Which Buddha are Buddhists talking about, and which Jesus are Christians talking about?

Accordingly, for the sake of clarity I shall use the term "historical Buddha" to refer to Siddhartha Gautama as reconstructed by historical scholarship that focuses mostly on the Pali Canon. Briefly Siddhartha Gautama, also known as Shakyamuni or "the Sage of the Shakya Clan," was born twenty-five years either side of 550 BCE, probably near the present town of Bodhgaya in northern India. His Hindu caste was Kshatriya ("warrior"), although he renounced the Hindu caste system. Since his father was a local raja he lived in relative wealth, which in his mid-twenties he found unsatisfactory. He married and fathered a son, abandoned his family, and entered what Hindu tradition calls the "forest hermit" stage of life to engage in a roughly six-year quest for satisfying answers to troubling boundary questions that arose because of his encounter with the "three marks of existence": old age, disease, and death.[1] Toward the end of this period, he tried extreme asceticism, which almost killed him, after which he engaged in a protracted period of meditation and experienced a breakthrough of consciousness, at which point he became known as "the Buddha" or "the Awakened One." He then began an approximately forty-year long career as an itinerant teacher, and gradually gathered together a community of monks supported by lay disciples—the first monastic community in the world's religions. He died of food poisoning at the age of eighty or eighty-one from a meal gathered from supporting lay disciples.

I shall use the term *Buddha of faith and practice* (in the sense of what the Noble Eightfold Path calls "right viewpoint" and "right aspiration") to refer to the doctrinal descriptions of the Buddha portrayed in the teachings and practices of the various schools and traditions of Buddhist meditative and devotional experience, and the schools of Buddhist philosophy.[2] The Buddha of faith and practice is an interpretation of the historical Buddha encountered in the "buddhaologies" of the various schools of Buddhist cumulative tradition. Therefore, the historical Buddha and the Buddha of faith and practice are interdependent, but they are not identical, and both are historical constructions.[3]

Likewise, throughout this book I shall use the term "historical Jesus" to mean "Jesus as reconstructed by historical scholarship," particularly by the Jesus Seminar and other Christian and non-Christian historians trying

---

1. According to the "life" of the Buddha as recounted in the *Jātakamāla* or "Birth Tales," Gautama encountered The Four Noble Sights while on four excursions to view gardens surrounding his palace: an old man, a diseased man, a dead man, and a wandering monk. Accordingly he vowed to take up the life of a wandering monk and search for solutions to the problems posed by the facts or "three marks of existence: old age, disease, and death. Essentially, this encounter is a conversion experience that began Gautama's quest for Awakening.

2. The Noble Eightfold Path is the Fourth Noble Truth: right viewpoint, right aspiration, right conduct, right speech, right livelihood, right effort, right concentration, and right mindfulness. The first Three Noble Truths are: all existence is suffering (*duhkha*), the cause of suffering is clinging to permanence (*tanha*), and release from suffering is possible.

3. There is no better introduction to Buddhist tradition in English print than R. L. F. Habito, *Experiencing Buddhism*.

to reconstruct the historical Jesus from canonical and noncanonical texts like the *Gospel of Thomas*. The historical Jesus was a Galilean Jewish peasant born in or near the village of Nazareth between 6 and 4 BCE, who around the age of thirty was baptized by John the Baptist. After his baptism, Jesus spent approximately a year traveling in Galilee as an itinerant teacher or rabbi, leading a band of disciples that included more than the twelve male disciples mentioned in the Gospels. Some, perhaps most, of his disciples were women.

He spent the last week of his life in Jerusalem preaching in and around the temple before Passover. As he had in Galilee, Jesus found avid listeners, which angered particularly the temple priests because they feared that the Roman occupying authorities could construe his popularity as rebellion against their control of Galilee and Judea. Because of his criticism of the temple priests and his attack on the money-changers in the temple, he was arrested by the temple leadership, charged with blasphemy and sedition, and handed over to the Roman military governor of Judea, Pontius Pilate, who ordered Jesus' execution by crucifixion around the year 30.

Jesus was baptized by John the Baptist, but he went far beyond John's apocalyptic preaching about the immanent reign of God. That is, when Jesus found his voice it was squarely within the Israelite/Judahite prophetic tradition's criticism of domination systems and their call for social and economic justice, which he connected with his own particular vision of the Kingdom or Commonwealth of God. Unlike John the Baptist, Jesus taught that the Commonwealth of God was immediately present in the struggle for justice on behalf of the poor and marginalized. For him, love and justice were two sides of the same coin. God, whom Jesus addressed as *Abba* or "Father," is experienced in loving relationships that engender nonviolent struggle for justice against the domination systems of his time. In particular, Jesus thought God's preferential option was decidedly for the poor. Finally, Jesus did not refer to himself as the Messiah.

I shall use the term *Jesus as the Christ* to mean "the Christ of faith" as portrayed in the four canonical gospels, the epistles of St. Paul and the writings of the rest of the New Testament, the Church's creeds and doctrines, and in Christian experience. The Christ of faith is a theological interpretation of the historical Jesus. The historical Jesus and the Christ of faith are of course interdependent, but they are not identical, and both are historical contructions.

I was first introduced to the historical Gautama and the Buddha of faith in 1960 in an undergraduate history of religions course at Chapman University. That same fall semester I was also enrolled in an Introduction to the New Testament course where I first encountered the historical Jesus and the Christ of faith. The high regard I have for the historical Buddha and the historical Jesus was first awakened in those days and continues to engage me in three ways.

First, the Buddha was a highly sophisticated teacher with profound insight into the structure of human existence. His teachings, which Buddhists call the Four Noble Truths—that all existence is implicated in impermanence and suffering (*duhkha*); that we cause suffering for ourselves and for other living beings by clinging (*tanha*) to permanence; that release from suffering is possible; that the Noble Eightfold Path is the practice that leads to the cessation of suffering and the achievement of Awakening (*nirvāna*)—ring true to my experiences. Yet I also think that because of evolutionary processes at play in the universe, human beings and other life forms suffer for reasons having little, if anything, to do with clinging to permanence.

Furthermore, economic domination systems like free-market capitalism bring great wealth to a small minority of individuals and nations at the cost of institutionalized poverty and environmental degradation for millions of persons oppressed by the wealthy few controlling the market. The suffering of the poor has very little to do with clinging to permanence. Institutionalized racism causing excruciating suffering to millions of people of color has little to do with clinging to permanence. The suffering experienced by women oppressed by patriarchal social and political domination systems has little to do with clinging to permanence. But even so, the Buddha's analysis of the human condition remains for me a pedagogical reality therapy, by which I mean that he accurately described important aspects of the human condition to which faithful Christians should pay attention.

Second, the Buddha's teaching concerning "non-self" (Pali, *anatta*; Sanskrit, *ānatman*) has helped me understand biblical images of human selfhood more accurately. I am certainly not the only Christian to have received such assistance. The Buddha's teaching about non-self is interdependent with his teaching about impermanence. All existing things and events, the Buddha taught, arise from ceaselessly changing interrelationships from moment to moment of their existence. But there is no permanent self-entity or "soul" remaining self-identical through time that *has* or *undergoes* these interdependent relationships. There exists only interdependent relationships undergoing ceaseless change and becoming. Or in more specifically Buddhist language, the processes of *pratītya-samuptpāda* or "interdependent co-arising" constitutes all things and events at every moment of space-time.

The doctrine of non-self constitutes a rejection of Hindu notions of an unchanging Self and serves as an axiom underlying every aspect of Buddhist teaching and meditative practice. Applied to human beings, non-self means that we are not embodiments of an unchanging self-entity or soul remaining self-identical through time. Buddhist teaching is firm in its rejection of notions of permanent selfhood and all doctrines of the soul. What "we" are, the Buddha taught, is a system of interdependent relationships—bodily, psychological, cultural, historical—that, in interdependence with everything else undergoing change and becoming in the universe, continuously creates "who" we are from moment to moment throughout our lifetimes. We are not permanent selves that "have" the relationships we experience and undergo; we *are* the relationships we experience as we experience them. We do not "have" our bodies and their functions; we *are* our bodies and their functions. We do not "have" hopes, fears, joys, sorrows, culture, history, friendships, family, wisdom, and ignorance; we *are* our hopes, fears, joys, sorrows, culture, history, friendships, family, wisdom, and ignorance as we experience them. Because these relationships are constantly changing, the "we" that they constitute is constantly changing. Consequently, the Buddha taught, permanent selfhood is an illusion the clinging to which causes suffering.

It was the Buddha's teaching about non-self and interdependent co-arising that opened my eyes to the Bible's understanding of selfhood. Stated in perhaps too summary a form, contemporary biblical scholarship has demonstrated that there exists no self–body dualism anywhere in the biblical texts.[4] For example, St. Paul translated Hebraic concepts from the Tanak, for example *nefesh* or "life" and *ru'ach* or "spirit" or "life force" into his portrayal of human selfhood as a unity of "soul" (*psyche*), "body" (*soma*), "flesh" (*sarx*), and "spirit" (*pneuma*) interdependently constituting the whole person throughout the moments of his or her life time. None of these elements can be separated from the total structure of a human being's existence because they are the interdependent relationships that make life

4. See Ingram, *The Modern Buddhist–Christian Dialogue*, chap. 7, for a more detailed comparison between Buddhist ad biblical paradigms of human selfhood.

"alive." Since again, according to St. Paul, God created human beings entire, in humanity's entirety human beings must be "redeemed."[5] The soul is not a Platonic immortal entity remaining self-identical through time. When a person dies, all the interdependent relationships constituting that person during his or her lifetime disappear. Or as Paul Tillich is reported as having said, "When you die, you die." So for St. Paul, resurrection is God's restoration of the whole person to a new embodied system of interdependent relationships that are in continuity with previous relationships before death. Faithful Christians, as he wrote in 1 Corinthians 15, participate in the resurrection of the historical Jesus as the Christ. Resurrection is not identical with Greek notions of the immortality of the human soul through which classical Christian theology since the third century read and translated, but inaccurately, Hebraic images of human selfhood.

Finally, the Buddha's emphasis on mediation and detachment are two aspects of his teachings that have opened me to the possibilities Christian contemplative practices.[6] As a Lutheran Christian, and so a member of a faith community in which Christian contemplative disciplines have been interpreted negatively as "works righteousness," I have found the Buddha's emphasis on meditation a truly liberating experience. Meditative detachment engenders "presence," and again I am not the first Christian for whom Buddhist meditative traditions have been helpful in this regard.[7] Like other Christians, I have incorporated Buddhist meditative practice, in my case the Zen discipline of *zazen* or "seated mediation," into my practice of contemplative payer as the starting point of my "interior" dialogue with Buddhism.

What I have learned most from the practice of *zazen* and contemplative prayer is that as long as you are consciousness of yourself, you can never fully concentrate on anything. Buddhist meditation and Christian contemplative prayer are exercises in the art of self-forgetfulness that allow us to be fully present to others as well as the interdependent processes of existence itself. As Shinryu Suzuki writes: "What I call 'I' is just a swinging door which moves when we inhale and when we exhale . . . [W]hen we become truly ourselves, we just become a swinging door, and we are purely

5. My interpretation of the Bible's selfhood paradigm is based on the following sources: von Rad, *Old Testament Theology*; Bornkamm, *Paul*; Bultmann, *Theology of the New Testament*, vol.2; and Ridderbos, *Paul: An Outline of His Theology*.

6. Ingram, "On the Practice of Faith."

7. See, for example, Johnston, *Christian Zen*.

independent of, and at the same time dependent upon everything."[8] Thomas Merton expressed a similar point of view from a Christian perspective: "Zen is the very awareness of the dynamism of life living itself in us—aware of itself in us, as being the one life that lives in us all."[9] Sitting in *zazen* or contemplative prayer has occasionally brought me to something like this awareness and has been an important corrective to the disconnected clutter of my conventional experiences.

## RETURNING

Since 1980 I have been an on-going participant in Buddhist-Christian dialogue as a member of the Society for Buddhist-Christian Studies. In similarity with many other Christians involved in this particular dialogue, Buddhism has deeply influenced my own theological reflection as a Lutheran process theologian. This experience is typical with Christians involved in dialogue with Buddhism, so typical that Buddhist practitioner Grace C. Buford was led to write an essay entitled, "If the Buddha is so Great, Why Are These People Christian?"[10] As a Lutheran Christian whose Buddhist friend, Mark Unno, has described as a "Lu-Bu," I think Buford's question requires a response. My particular answer is that it is possible to be a "Christian and a Buddhist, too," as process theologian John Cobb has written.[11] But, of course, one must be careful to spell out what this means.

My dialogue with he historical Gautama the Buddha and the Buddha of faith and practice is one example of what John S. Dunne described as a process of "passing over and returning," which I have appropriated as a means of structuring five of the chapters of this book.[12] John Cobb describes the dynamics of passing over and returning as a process of "going beyond dialogue." In his view, passing "beyond dialogue" does not mean that the dialogue needs to stop. Ideally, the practice of theological reflection is a continuing dialogical engagement with the world's religious traditions and with the natural sciences. But the phrase "beyond dialogue" is Cobb's way of naming what Dunne refers to as "returning." Thus going beyond dialogue implies continually engaging *in* dialogue as part of one's continual

8. Suzuki, *Zen Mind, Beginner's Mind*, 29.

9. Merton, *Mystics and Zen Masters*, 21–22.

10. Buford, "If the Buddha Is so Great, Why Are These People Christians?"

11. Cobb, "Can a Christian Be a Buddhist, Too?"

12. Dunne, *The Way of All the Earth*, chap. 1.

growth in Christian faith. Cobb assumes that the same process occurs for non-Christians engaged in dialogue with Christian tradition.[13]

As a Lutheran historian of religions engaged in theological reflection, my dialogue with the world's religious traditions in general, and Buddhism in particular, has taken me beyond the conventional boundaries of Christian faith and practice into non-Christian teachings and experience, wherein I have learned and appropriated truths I think I have perceived. This movement has been followed by a "return" to the "home" of my Lutheran brand of Christian faith and practice—enriched, renewed, and I hope creatively transformed.

So the dialectic of passing over and returning has been part of my theological reflection for fifty years, and, I think, it describes the experiences of most Christians engaged in interreligious dialogue.[14] And while many Christians and Buddhists have not returned to the home of their own traditions after undertaking the adventure of dialogue, and while some Buddhists and Christians now identify themselves as "Christian-Buddhists" or Buddhist-Christians," I find myself increasingly convinced of the truth of Christian faith and practice even as I am convinced of the truth of Buddhist faith and practice.

I do not mean that I find everything in Christian tradition of value, particularly the theological imperialism of Christian fundamentalism and much evangelical neo-orthodoxy. Nor do I think everything that wears a Buddhist label is in harmony with the Buddha's teachings. The practice of dialogue does not mean being uncritical about the truth claims of any religious tradition, including one's own. Furthermore, some aspects of Buddhist doctrine and some elements of Christian doctrine are incommensurable: for example, Buddhist nontheism and Christian monotheism, or the Buddha's emphasis on self-effort as necessary for the achievement of Awakening and the Pauline, Augustinian, Lutheran, Calvinist doctrines of justification by grace through faith alone.

So even as I continue to think that monotheism offers the most coherent interpretation of how the universe works in light of what contemporary scientific cosmology and evolutionary biology have revealed about the natural forces at play in nature, I also have Buddhist friends who argue

13. Cobb, *Beyond Dialogue*, chap. 3.

14. For example, see Lew, "Becoming Who You Always Were: The Story of a Zen Rabbi"; Lubarsky, "Enriching Awareness: A Jewish Encounter with Buddhism"; Cobb, "Contacts with Buddhism: A Christian Confession"; Jonas, "Loving Someone You Can't See"; and M. R. Habito, "On Becoming a Buddhist Christian."

that contemporary scientific cosmology support's Buddhism's nontheistic worldview. For this reason alone, the natural sciences need to be brought into the practice of conceptual interreligious dialogue as a "third partner."[15]

Furthermore, sociological factors play a profound role in one's religious or nonreligious identity. Chances are, had I been born in Saudi Arabia or Kuwait, I would be a Sunni Muslim. Had I been born in Sri Lanka or Tibet, chances are I would be a Buddhist. Had I been born in Ireland, Spain, or Italy chances are I would be a Roman Catholic. Certainly, cultural factors do not *determine* one's religious identity; I am not a sociological determinist. Persons can and do move from one inherited religious identity to another and some persons experience plural religious identities. In all these choices available to contemporary human beings, sociological, cultural, and historical factors certainly play a transformative role in the experiences of faithful religious persons in all traditions.[16] So my particular identity as a Lutheran Christian is contextualized by the accident of my birth in the postmodern, technologically sophisticated, religiously plural, consumerist culture of the United States.

Furthermore, while it may not be quite correct to claim that "truth is relative," the religious claims to which persons commit themselves are constructed and "relational" in the sense that we can only experience and know anything from the historical, cultural, and gender contexts we occupy at moment we claim to know anything. An important conclusion that I draw from these assumptions is that I cannot claim that my conclusion that "a Christian can be a theological pluralist, too" is normative for anyone other than me. I can only reasonably speak from my own experiences and hope it helps others with their theological reflection.

So why am I a Lutheran Christian given my veneration of the historical Buddha? The Buddha's teaching about meditative detachment as a means of living fully in the present without illusory pretenses seem true to my experiences. Many of these experiences are painful, which means that waking up to the interdependent structures of existence as they are engenders compassionate interaction with all living things, which in turn is the foundation of what the Vietnamese Buddhist monk, Thich Nhat Hanh, called "social engagement."[17] The Buddha's path to liberation—acting without

15. See Ingram, *Buddhist–Christian Dialogue in an Age of Science*, chapt. 1

16. See Berger, *The Heretical Imperative*, for an important analysis of religious faith in the contemporary world from the perspective of sociology of knowledge.

17. Nhat Hahn, *Being Peace*.

desire for personal success with good will toward all living beings—creates a form of non-ego-centered consciousness that can deal with life's rough-and-tumble without pretenses. Such consciousness can produce marvelous social outcomes. Similar experiences are engendered by the practice of Franciscan, Jesuit, and Benedictine contemplative disciplines. It was my interior dialogue with Zen Buddhist meditative practice that gave me access to the contemplative practices of Christianity, the practice of which leads to experiences and social results quite similar to Buddhist tradition.

But I have never attained the radical self-sufficiency upon which the Buddha insisted. "Be lamps unto yourself," he taught. According to the *Digha-nikāya*, which contains some of the earliest texts in the Buddhist Canon, his last instruction to his disciples was:

> You should live as lamps unto yourselves, being your own refuge, seeking no other refuge; with the Dhamma as an island, with the Dhamma as your refuge, seeking no other refuge . . . Those monks in my time or afterwards live thus, seeking an island of refuge in themselves and the Dhamma and nowhere else, these zealous monks are my monks and will overcome the darkness (of rebirth).[18]

In other words, the structure of Buddhist experience and the structure of Christian experience are different. While Christians sometimes experience the Buddha as an Awakened one, Buddhists seem unable to experience the historical Jesus as the Christ because of the specifics of the Buddhist path and the way this path fleshes our in the experiences of faithful Buddhists. Buddhist tradition seems much more worldview specific in this regard than Christian tradition.

I do not mean that Buddhist tradition is inferior to Christian tradition. Nor do I think that religious imperialism is inherently part of Buddhism or Christianity, which is not to say that there have not existed imperialist Buddhists or Christians. My intention is descriptive; I am suggesting that the structure of Buddhist experience and the structure of Christian experience are different, even though there are similarities. Given that I am a Lutheran, the structure of my experience is more like St. Paul's: "For I do not do what I want but I do everything I hate"; and "I do not do the good I want, but the evil I do not want is what I do" (Rom 7:15, 19). Bonnie Thurston's description of St. Paul's experience also reflects my own:

18. Cited in Schumann, *The Historical Buddha*, 246.

In the struggle to be a lamp unto myself, I am brought face to face with Jesus Christ. There are many points of comparison between the Buddha and the Christ, and many helpful comparisons have been drawn. I want to focus on one that I have not seen: the attitude of each toward his followers. The Buddha says, "be lamps unto yourself" and "one is one's own refuge." The Christ says, "Come to me all that are weary and are carrying heavy burdens, and I will give you rest." (Matt 11:28)[19]

I know from experience my own inability to be a lamp unto myself. Of course, lack of self-discipline and personal ignorance play a part in my experiences, as anyone who knows me can attest. But something internal always seems to block my attempts to attain the self-fulfillment the Buddha called "Awakening." The Christian word that labels this "something" is "sin." Sin is not simply immoral action, but rather names the personal and collective egoism that is ontologically ingredient in the structure of human existence that separates us from God, each other, and the life forms with which we must live on this planet. That is, sin is constituted by grasping for permanent selfhood, according to which individuals and communities behave as if they are the center of the universe, at the level of biology a process Charles Darwin described as "survival of the fittest." Or restated in the language of process theology, sin is placing one's own subjective aim for one's self over God's initial aim that we achieve the maximum intensity of harmonious interrelationships with all human and nonhuman life, "harmony" meaning a whole that is greater than the sum of its parts.

To my way of thinking, then, sin is an individual and communal expression of what Buddhists call *tāṇha*, the egoism of trying to prove to ourselves that we are permanent selves, from which we cannot free ourselves through any form of self-effort. Sin is therefore a source of much human suffering and the suffering experienced by other life forms on this planet. All one has to do to confirm empirically that sin is ontologically ingredient in the structure of human existence is read a daily newspaper or watch the news on television. So given my personal experiential confirmation of the reality of sin, my experience has taught me that taking refuge in myself is an illusion because here is no permanent self in which to take refuge. I need to take refuge in, that is, trust a reality operating externally to myself and yet is part of my self, a reality Christians name "grace."

19. Thurston, "The Buddha Offered Me a Raft," 124,

The source of grace is God's universal love for all things and events caught in the field of space-time, which Christian faith apprehends incarnated in the historical Jesus as the Christ of faith. It is through grace that God interacts with us and with everything else in the universe at every moment of space-tine since the first moment of space-time at the Big Bang. The primary source of my understanding of God's graceful character is, to be sure, what I have learned from the history of Christian theological reflection as this has fleshed out in my own experiences. But I have also learned much about grace from Jewish and Islamic tradition, as well as the thirteenth-century writings of Shinran, the founder of the True Pure Land School of Buddhism (*Jōdō Shinshū*), known popularly as Shin Buddhism.[20]

Many of the details of Shinran's life remain unclear, although most scholars accept the following biographical outline. He was born in Kyōto, then known as Heian-kyō, in 1173. When he was in his teens, his father, Hino Arinori, decided he should enter the Tendai monasteries on Mount Hiei, where for the next twenty years he studied every form of Buddhist philosophy and practice available in the twelfth century. His chief preoccupation during his years as a monk involved a question that was the focus of most Japanese Buddhists at the time: how could he attain certainty that the achievement of Awakening was a possibility for him or anyone else born in the age *mappō* or "end of the Dharma."

According to a number of Buddhist texts, including the *Lotus Sutra*, which is the textual foundation of the Tendai traditions of Buddhism, the universe continually revolves through three stages: (1) the age of *shōbō* or "True Dharma," which is an age initiated by the appearance of a Buddha in history and lasts either 500 years or 1,000 years, depending on which Buddhist text one is reading; (2) the age of *zōpō* or "counterfeit doctrine," lasting 1000 years; and (4) the age of *mappō* lasting ten thousand years, after which a new Buddha appears in history and the cycle starts over again. During the age of "True Dharma," when the influence of a historical Buddha is at its height, the last historical Buddha being Gautama the Buddha, Awakening is achievable because persons born into this age are able to "be lamps unto themselves" and achieve Awakening through their own "self-efforts" or "self-power" (Japanese, *jiriki*) through the discipline of meditation. But as a world cycle spins in to an age of "counterfeit doctrine," the influence of a historical Buddha diminishes because beings born into this age are born with diminished intellectual, moral, and physical capacities. Consequently,

20. See Ingram, *The Dharma of Faith*.

very few persons attain Awakening through the "self-effort" or "self-power" required of followers the Buddha's teachings. Finally, a world cycle runs down into the age of *mappō*, the age lasting for another 10,000 years. Persons born in this age are born with capacities so damaged that no one can attain Awakening through any self-powered practice because the Dharma itself is so diminished that no one is able to practice the Buddha's teachings, even monks or nuns, by means of the traditional practice of Buddhism. It is impossible to be a "lamp unto oneself" in an age of *mappō* because what was available to persons during an age of True Dharma is no longer available in this age. But world-cycles continuously spin, and a new age of True Dharma begins at the end of an age of *mappō* with the appearance of a new historical Buddha, the next expected historical Buddha being Meitreya (Japanese, Miroku).

As a monk who threw himself into every form of mediation available to him as he mastered the complex doctrinal traditions of the Buddhist Canon, Shinran never found assurance that Awakening was possible for him or anyone else. Then as he studied the texts of the Pure Land tradition focused on veneration of Amida Buddha (The Buddha of Infinite Light), he found what he was looking for and left the monastery, renounced his vows, married an ex-nun, raised a family, and spent the rest of his life until his death in 1258 teaching, organizing his followers, and writing numerous treatises spelling out his particular Pure Land teachings. What Shinran found can be summarized as "Awakening by faith through the 'other-power' of Amida Buddha alone."[21]

For Shinran, human nature is so corrupted by the fact of rebirth in the present age of *mappō* that no one can be a lamp unto himself or herself by means of the self-powered practices of Buddhism. The only option is to rely on the "other-power" of Amida Buddha. Such reliance is not the self-powered act to trust Amida, but is an unmerited gift transferred to faithful persons by Amida's compassionate other-power (*tariki*). One is thereby empowered to live compassionately in the world, free from the anxiety of self-efforted attempts to achieve what one thinks one does not already have. At death, faithful persons are reborn into Amida Buddha's Buddha Land, called the Pure Land, *as* Awakened Buddhas. In other words, even Awakening is a gift of Amida's graceful other-power.

21. For a more detailed discussion see Ingram, "Shinran Shōnin and Martin Luther: A Soteriological Comparison."

The experience of "other-power" and the experience of "grace" in Shin Buddhism and mainline Protestant theology are structurally similar. So is the meaning of "faith" in Shin Buddhism and mainline Protestant theology, where faith is defined as trust in Amida Buddha and, in Protestant theology, trust in God. Of course, "sin" and *mappō* are not identical concepts, and the concept of *mappō* does not play the same role in contemporary Shin Buddhist thought as it did for Shinran. Even so, faith in both Shin Buddhist and Protestant Christian tradition entails non-trust in one's own self-efforts. Which is not to say that Shinran was the "Luther of Japan." Japanese Pure Land Buddhism and Protestant, particularly Lutheran, doctrines of grace and faith may point to structurally similar experiences, but the objects of Pure Land faith and Christian faith are not identical. Amida Buddha is a bodhisattva, not God. Still, an experiential doorway exists where Buddhists and Christians can meet in interreligious dialogue.

In all probability, what I have written in the above paragraphs is perhaps too "confessional" for a Lutheran scholar of the history of religions. My views on grace should not be uncritically universalized. In fact, I think what Buddhists experience as Awakening has happened and still happens to the Buddha's disciples. But I also think that what most Buddhists experience as Awakening and what Christians experience as redemption are not identical, which does not imply that Awakening and redemption are incommensurable experiences or concepts. I tend to understand the Buddha's teaching regarding Awakening and Christian teaching about redemption as complementary concepts pointing to similar, but not necessarily identical, experiences—in the sense of the conclusion of the Epistle of James that "faith without works is dead" (2:26).

What I mean is that the historical Gautama the Buddha helps me focus on the realities of existence. So does the historical Jesus, especially in his teaching that God's love favors the poor and the oppressed. In this sense I am a Christian and a Buddhist, too. But it is in Jesus as the Christ of faith that I apprehend the source of grace that I think overflows this universe like a waterfall. Which does not mean that non-Christians do not experience grace through their distinctive traditions and practices. But however experienced, grace is a gift from God offered to all human beings regardless of the religious or secular labels they wear—as well as to everything that lives—that frees us from having to be anxious about our awakening or redemption so that we can give full attention to the practice of "loving/

compassionate wisdom" without regard to achieving something we think we lack, as if we are on the outside of our lives looking in.[22]

Wisdom, in both the Buddha's teachings and in Christian mystical theology, is the experience of the utter interdependency of all things and events at every moment of space-time. The Buddha's teachings were focused on disciplines meant to engender the experience of interdependence and non-self. Interdependence is also asserted in the Christian doctrines of creation and incarnation as this is understood through the lenses of the Prologue to the Gospel of John and confirmed in the experience of Christian faith. The experience of universal interdependence is the source of compassionate love—where compassion is experiencing the suffering of all sentient beings as one's own because it is; and where love means socially engaged action in the world's rough-and-tumble struggle for peace and justice with utter disregard for one's own self-fulfillment, for there is no "self" to fulfill. Or as the historical Jesus is reported as having said, "For those who want to save their lives will lose it, and those who lose their life for my sake . . . will save it" (Mark 8:35).

22. See Ingram, *Wrestling with the Ox*, 126–31, for a fuller explanation of what I mean by "loving/compassionate wisdom" as the practice of faith.

# 6

## A Question of Balance

*Confucius and "Philosophical Daoism"*

### PASSING OVER

CHINA IS ONE OF the oldest continuous civilization on Earth. The very first Chinese dynasties, long thought of as legendary, are now being confirmed as historical.[1] The concept of "China" itself began with the first emperor, Qin Shi Huangdi, who in 221 BCE conquered several smaller kingdoms to form a unified state. This new kingdom was called *Zhongguo*, the "Middle Kingdom," still the Chinese name for China and which symbolizes its mythology of geographic and cosmic centrality. It was also referred to as *Tian Xia*, "Under Heaven," which indicates that China's collective self-conception was fundamentally religious.

Chinese religious history displays an incredible diversity. For example, the capital of China during the Tang Dynasty (618–907) was at that time the largest city in the world. Zoroastrians, Nestorian Christians, Manicheans, Muslims, and Buddhists all lived together in relative harmony under the authority of the emperor. Later, the Chinese were exposed to Judaism, Catholicism, and Protestantism. But each of these religions were regarded by China's ruling class and the Confucian government bureaucracy as "barbarian," meaning "foreign." Which means that even though foreign religions were tolerated, they did not become structurally part of the pluralism ingredient in the indigenous Chinese religion traditions. This

---

1. Archaeology in China is in its infancy compared to that in Egypt, for example; and new finds are periodically putting the earliest dates of Chinese civilization farther and farther into the past.

is so because the worldview supporting Chinese religious pluralism focuses on the rhythm of agricultural cycles, the primacy of the family, and the structure of community as a collection of families.

The beginnings of Chinese religious history can be traced back to China's first three dynasties: the Xia, the Shang, and the Zhou. The Xia Dynasty was the time of mythological culture heroes: Fu Xi first established the centrality of the family; Shen Nong invented agriculture; Huang Di, the Yellow Emperor, created medicine. At this moment, however, there is no archaeological evidence confirming the existence of the Xia Dynasty.

But there is evidence that the Shang Dynasty was founded around 1600 BCE in the present-day Yellow River Valley. The Shang Dynasty was a theocracy based not on military might but on religious ritual. The ruler was a priest-king who had power to communicate with the sky god, Di. Like many other civilizations around the world, the Shang Dynasty engaged in human and animal sacrifice as a form of transaction in which offerings of meat, grain, or wine were offered to deities in hopes of obtaining immediate or long-range personal and communal benefits. Important persons were buried with texts, food, jewels, and sculpted human figures. Today, sacrifice is carried on in community temple services in the form of fruit, foodstuffs, and incense offerings.

Another hallmark of Chinese religions from prehistory until today is divination. Evidence from the Late Shang indicates that rulers used divination in interpreting the patterns of cracks on the bones of oxen and turtle shells to predict the future. When the Zhou Dynasty overthrew the Shang Dynasty, besides ending the practice of human sacrifice, the Zhou kings introduced a new form of divination. By randomly picking from a pile of stalks of the milfoil plant, the diviner would generate odd or even numbers, which when repeated several times, would turn into a series of broken or unbroken lines. A diagram of six lines made up a hexagram. The text that interpreted the meaning of sixty-four of these hexagrams was called the *Yijing*, or "Book of Changes," more commonly known in the West as the *I Ching*.[2]

The *Yijing* is grounded in a metaphysics that links human action to cosmic cycles that are continuously changing. It was consulted by emperors, fortune-tellers, and common folk and was appropriated by Confucians, Daoists, and Buddhists. In more contemporary times, the *Yijing* has also become popular as part of Western counterculture. In China today,

2. See Wilhelm, *Change: Eight Lectures on the I Ching*.

consulting the *Yijing* is technically illegal, though prevalent, and it is still studied academically.

Related to divination and sacrifice is ancestor reverence. Ancestors were asked about which sacrifice was appropriate, and they were also asked to predict the future. They also served as the protectors of families from natural and human-caused calamities. Community deities were also consulted about issues that affected the larger community beyond the family. Evidence of ancestor reverence can be found in burial practices dating from Neolithic times and is still an ingredient in contemporary Chinese religious practice. The more archaeological evidence has uncovered, the more support has been found for the hypothesis that ancestral reverence is one of the few constants of Chinese civilization from earliest times to the present. Ancestor reverence is a demonstration of the mutual dependency between the living and the dead. The dead have more power than when alive, but need supplies and sacrifice only the living can provide; the living need protection.

Since there is no concept of an immortal soul in traditional Chinese religion, what then is addressed in ancestor reverence? Traditional Chinese religion holds that human beings have several kinds of "spirits" or "souls" (or energies) that cluster together to form every human being. The *po* soul, which is *yin,* is physical energy that at death disperses back to the Earth, also identified as *yin.* The *hun* soul denotes non-physical mental energies and are equated with *yang,* which can be stored in ancestral tablets and remain part of the family lineage. From a sociological perspective, the family community—not the Western nuclear Western family—includes all persons with the same surname as well as dead relatives. The Chinese family is more like a "lineage corporation" and is the religious institution upon which all other Chinese communal religious institutions and practices are patterned.

Around 1050 BCE the Zhou kingdom established a dynasty by conquering the Shang kingdom. Sacrificial rites were conducted by shamans. Men or women could be possessed by spirits or in trances journey to the abodes of deities to receive instructions or deliver messages or requests from human beings. Shamans were also healers and could consult with the ancestors. Emperors used them right up until their suppression in the eleventh century. In fact, many Chinese religions have their origins in shamanistic practices, from the Heavenly Master Daoists of the third century CE to the Taiping Rebellion in the nineteenth century. Several spirit-writing cults active in Hong Kong today are also based on revelations from shamanic figures.

The Warring States Period (403–221 BCE) of the Eastern Zhou Dynasty (770–221) was a time of almost constant civil warfare and political disunity. The Zhou kings had little real power and rival states engaged in almost constant warfare in an attempt to force all of China under their control. The Warring States Period was also the time in which the classical traditions of Chinese philosophy and religion originated as answers to the question, "How can human beings learn to live together in peace and harmony?" during a time when human beings were *not* living together peacefully and harmoniously. Most of the classical schools of Chinese philosophy and religion are best understood as social-political-ethical philosophies of religion focused on this question. This is certainly the case with Confucius' teachings. In his time, advocates of different schools traveled from court to court advocating their own political-religious philosophies as the solution to the chaos of the times while denigrating their rivals. This era has popularly been referred to as the Hundred Schools Period (551–233). The schools included logicians, hedonists, advocates of "universal love without distinctions," known in the West as Moism, and the cynical statesmanship of Legalism or Fa Chia. Sunzi, the military strategist who wrote *The Art of War*,[3] also dates from this period. The two religious-philosophical systems of this period that continue to deeply influence Chinese philosophy and religion are Daoism and Confucianism.

The Confucian tradition has shaped the ethical and ritual norms of China for more than two millennia. Its founder, Kongzi (551–479), better known today by his Latinized name as "Confucius," was born twenty-five years either side of 551 BCE, which means he was roughly a contemporary of Gautama the Buddha. He was a minor official in the state of Lu who became a teacher. After his death, Confucius's first and second generation disciples compiled his sayings into a book of 497 verses in twenty chapters known as the *Lunyu*, or in English, the *Analects*.[4]

As the *Analects* reveals, Confucius' teachings are in direct relation to the social, political, and ethical chaos the Chinese people confronted during the later half of the period of the Warring States. As previously noted,

3. See Cleary, trans., *The Art of War*.

4. See Waley, *The Analects of Confucius*, for a good introduction to Confucius' teachings and an excellent translation of the *Analects*. Also see Ching, *Chinese Religions*, chaps. 1–2, for an excellent introduction to Confucius' teachings.

the fundamental question both the Confucius and the Daoist masters sought to answer was: "How can human beings learn to live together in peace and community? Confucius spent about fifteen years as an itinerant teacher trying to convince politicians and warlords to accept his solution to bringing order out of the chaos of the times. He was unable to convince any politician to accept his ideas as the best means for reestablishing a just and ordered state, so he retired to his hometown and quietly taught anyone who wanted to follow his Way (*dao*). He died in 479 BCE believing that he was a failure because no state accepted his views as their state philosophy.

Since both Confucius' teachings and "Philosophical Daoism" are interpretations of the worldview underlying Chinese religion and philosophy, art, architecture, technology, politics, and everything else traditionally "Chinese," it would be well to specify the elements of this worldview, whose best known textual source in the West is the *Dao De Ching*, or "Classic on the Way and Its Power"[5]

The most literal English translations of *dao* are "way," "path," or "road," but the essential meaning is "Way." All the nuanced meanings of *dao* are metaphorical expansions of "Way." Thus *dao* can mean the defining character of a craft, skill, or discipline. For example, becoming a master architect requires mastery of the defining principles or the *dao* of architecture as one applies these defining principles to creating buildings that are in harmony with their environments as well as being both beautiful and functional. Learning a martial art requires mastering the principles or *dao* of a particular martial skill like the Korean art of Taekwondo ("foot-hand way") or the Japanese martial arts of Jūdō ("gentle way") or Kendō ("way of the sword"). Basically, learning to achieve mastery of any skill or craft requires mastering the defining *dao* of that skill of craft.

The *Dao De Ching's* portrayal of the *dao* metaphorically extends the literal meaning of "Way" in three interdependent ways. First, the word *dao* means "the way of ultimate reality." In this sense, the *dao* cannot be perceived, for it exceeds all the senses. It is nameless and formless, and yet it is the foundation of all names and forms. It transcends all definition,

---

5. Tradition has it that the *Dao De Ching* was written by Laozi, meaning "old teacher" or "old man." But most scholars doubt that Laozi was the author or that he was a historical human being since detailed textual analysis of the *Dao De Ching* reveals that it is an anthology of Daoist sayings from different periods of Philosophical Daoism's history. Several legends concerning Laozi seem to support this view, e.g., his visit to India where he taught the Buddha. For excellent overviews of Daoist tradition, see Welch, *The Way and Its Power*. Also see Waley, *The Parting of the Way*.

description, and conceptualization. Or as the first chapter of the *Dao De Ching* has it, "The Way that can be talked about is not the Way."[6] *Dao* in the sense of ultimate reality can only be known by experience, the way a thirsty person in the Mohave Desert knows how cold water quenches thirst only by drinking cold water, or the way lovers know what love is only by experiencing and giving love. Linguistic description may point to—but never capture—the Dao, just as words might point to but never capture the experience of quenching one's thirst or experiencing love. The *Dao* can only be experientially apprehended through apophatic "mystical insight" that is the goal of disciplined meditative practice in all religions cross-culturally.

Second, *dao* means "the way of the universe," as symbolized by this well-known symbol.

The left half of the circle is called *yin* and the right side *yang*. *Yin* is energy that is feminine, dark, negative, death, and so forth, while *yang* is energy that is masculine, light, positive, life, and so forth. The circle is bisected by a wavy line, not a straight line; nature never goes in a straight line but wiggles between the polar energies of *yin* and *yang*. On the *yin* side of the circle there is a black dot of *yang*, and on the *yang* side there is a light dot of *yin*. Nothing is completely *yin* or *yang*.

In other words, the natural forces of the universe are a balancing act between *yin* and *yang* forces; every thing and event naturally seeks to balance or harmonize polar opposite forms of energy. As stated in chapter 2 of the *Dao De Ching*:

6. My paraphrase of Waley's translation, "The Way that can be told of is not the Unvarying Way." See *The Way and Its Power*, 141.

It is because every one under Heaven recognizes beauty as beauty,
   that the idea of ugliness exists.
And equally, if every one recognized virtue as virtue, this would
   merely create fresh conceptions of wickedness.
For truly Being and Not-being grow out of one another;
Difficult and easy complete one another.
Long and short test one another;
High and low determine one another.
Front and back give sequence to one another.
Therefore the Sage relies on actionless activity,
Carries on Wordless teaching,
But the myriad of creatures are worked upon by him: he does not
   disown them.[7]

Yet what is a harmonious balance at one point in time may not be at another point in time. The line bisecting the symbol of the *doo* is a curving line, not a Euclidian straight line between two points. As noted, nature never goes in straight lines, but wiggles between bipolar forces. Which means existence is a balancing act between ever-shifting bipolar forces everywhere at all times and in all places. Thus whenever any thing or event becomes too *yang*-like, an opposite *yin* force is generated that pulls that thing or event toward a point of harmonious balance between *yin* and *yang*. For too much of one thing becomes self-destructive. So for example, too much justice becomes a tyranny, while too much love becomes mere soap-opera sentimentality. Life depends on a balance of *yin* and *yang*; too much heat is destructive, as is too much cold. At the summer solstice, the height of *yang*, the seasons revolve toward the winter solstice, which is the height of *yin*. Everything in nature happens because of the ebb and flow of *yin* and *yang* energies seeking balance between polar opposites.

The third meaning of the *dao* is the way human beings should live in accordance with the ebb and flow of *yin* and *yang* energies, or perhaps better, "fields" of energy. All living things, other than human beings, naturally live in accord with the *dao*, meaning living in harmony with the ever-shifting flowing of *yin* and *yang*. But human beings have egos which we incessantly impose on natural processes to make them conform to our desires. Such attempts are "unnatural" and cause much suffering to human beings as well as to non-human life forms because they place us out of harmony with the *dao*. So human beings must train themselves to live naturally; living in harmony with the *dao* is something human beings must learn. To this

7. Ibid., 143.

end, the *Dao De Ching* prescribes a disciplined life style called *wu-wei* or "actionless action," or "action without action" that reflects the movements of *yin* and *yang* in our lives.

It needs to be noted that *wu-wei* is not "in-action," but rather action without the assertion of ego in action, without attachment to the fruits or results of action. It is remaining passive as one allows the *dao* to work through one's life. The most important symbol for an "actionless action" life-style is water. Not water, for example in a swamp—although this form of water is certainly creative—but free flowing water. Or as chapter 73 of the *Dao De Ching* describes it:

> Nothing under heaven is softer or more yielding than water; but when it attacks things hard and resistant there is not one of them that can prevail. For they can find no way of altering it. That the yielding conquers the resistant and the soft conquers the hard is a fact known by all [human beings], yet utilized by none.[8]

So *wu-wei* essentially means the non-assertion of ego in action. That is, we must train ourselves, primarily through systems of meditation and physical discipline, to let go of all ego-centered desires to make nature conform to our wills so that we become who we are naturally formed by the *dao's* processes. Thus as we gradually do nothing, the *dao* gradually does everything. In the process, we acquire *de* or "power," or more accurately, "the power of virtue."

Philosophical Daoism had important political implications because it arose as an answer to the social and political anarchy of the the Warring States Period. Nothing, Philosophical Daoism asserted, is so unnatural as governmental systems. Governments are unnatural because they are systems that force the majority of human beings to live in accordance with the collective egos of powerful political elites imposing their standards on the rest of the community. It is governments that start wars, create poverty, and oppress the majority of human beings by forcing them to act unnaturally, meaning out of harmony with the *dao*. Thus rulers and politicians should govern by non-governing, so that what is natural for the evolution of human community can gradually evolve and communal life in harmony with the *dao* naturally emerge.

"Actionless action" is the opposite of Confucius' answer to how persons should live in harmony with the *dao*. Where Confucius proposed a

8. Ibid., 238.

system of values, the purpose of which is to create an ordered and humane society, Philosophical Daoism proposed an inner transformation of character from which a humane commonwealth based on ethical behavior would flow naturally, like water flowing down a river flows naturally. It should be noted that both Philosophical Daoism and Confucius assumed that human nature, as a reflection of the *dao,* is naturally good. Human actions guided by ignorance of the *dao* are self-destructive and harmful to the human community and to nature.

While Confucius' teachings assumed the first two meanings of the word *dao* described above, he differed from the philosophical Daoists about how human beings should live in harmony with the *dao.* Confucian tradition is a Way of activist social engagement; Daoist tradition is a Way of social withdrawal and mysticism. This contrast is readily seen in the *Analects.*[9] According to this text, Confucius taught that living in harmony with the *dao* required becoming a "Superior Human Being," meaning a Sage who has learned to live at the ever-shifting points of balance between extremes, and in so doing is like a good host who is able to put others at their ease by knowing what to do in any social or political situation—and doing it. The defining marks of the Superior Human being are: "ritual" (*ri*), "humanity" (*ren*), "filial piety" (*hsiao*), the "rectification of names" (*meng*), "doctrine of the mean" (*chung-yung*), and "culture" (*wen*).

The Chinese word for "ritual" is *ri* and originates in the Chinese ancestor traditions that predate Confucius by fifteen hundred years. Rituals were performed at the funeral rites for dead family members so that their *yun* energy, which is *yang,* would be free so that it could exist as an ancestor working for the welfare of living family members. A family's failure to perform funeral rituals on a regular cycle resulted in transforming the dead ancestor's yang-soul into a "hungry ghost" or *quei,* who retaliated against the living because of the lack of ritual respect of a neglectful family. Confucius maintained this original meaning and added to it his own ethical and social interpretations.

First, for Confucius "ritual" also meant "etiquette" in the French meaning of this term: the rules of social conduct and intercourse that publically display the distinctiveness of human nature and social togetherness. In this sense, the Superior Human Being knows what to do in every social situation and thereby knows how to put others at their ease. Second, "ritual" for Confucius also meant the actual public performance of the rules governing

9. See Waley, *The Analects of Confucius.*

communal interaction, the result of which is the creation of social harmony that is a reflection of the balance between yin *and* yang. In other words, the Superior Human Being knows what to do (the rules of etiquette) and publically performs the rules of etiquette in all social and communal situations, which is the meaning of "ritual."

*Ren* means "humanity," "benevolence," "virtue." "Humanity" is the theme around which all of Confucius' teachings revolved. The Superior Human Being has trained himself or herself to apprehend the common humanity all persons share that defines all human beings as "human" and distinguishes human beings from all other forms of living beings, and treats all persons accordingly. Like all things and events, human beings are a reflection of the ever-flowing energy of the *dao*. So "humanity" is the realization that all human beings are particular interconnected and interdependent expressions of the *dao* and therefore should be interacted with accordingly.

"Filial Piety" refers to the concrete ethical expression of "humanity" in communal interaction through the "five filial relationships": (1) father and son, (2) husband and wife, (3) elder brother and junior brother, (4) elder friend and junior friend, (5) ruler and subject. Note that what defines the superior/inferior relationship is age and gender: generally, Confucius and subsequent Confucian tradition taught that males are socially superior to females, and older people are socially superior to younger people. Also, Confucius identified the superior side of the relationship as *yang* and the inferior side as *yin*, a notion that is *not* found in Philosophical Daoism. This thereby makes Confucius' teachings highly patriarchal, which again is not the case with Philosophical Daoism.

So fathers (or mothers, or parents) have obligations to their children that must be fulfilled, which are created by the very fact of having children: basically to see to the protection, education, and welfare of their children. For what sons particularly, but also daughters, receive from fathers or parents, children have the obligation to be obedient to the father's or parental authority even after they become married adults raising their own families. Likewise, elder brothers have obligations to look after and be examples for a younger brother's conduct, while younger brothers have the duty to be obedient and respectful to elder brothers. The same is true for the elder sister/younger sister relationship. Similar superior/inferior responsibilities occur in the relationship between elder friends and junior friends. Finally, for what rulers do to bring order and stability into a society by keeping the forces that cause social chaos and disharmony at bay, subjects owe submission and obedience to the ruler's authority. Since everyone is in either a superior or inferior social relationship to someone in any community—because one is always older and younger and male and female—knowing *what* to do (etiquette) and publically doing it through a display of socially constructed rituals creates social harmony that is reflective of the *dao.* Superior Human Beings, motivated by humanity, teach "humanity" to others by their public display of filial piety.

The "rectification of names" refers to the disciplined use of language. Our sense of reality, the way things really are, is a largely a linguistic construction. For example, the meaning of realities such as "death," "life," "old age," "truth," or, in Confucius' case, the *dao,* is something human beings construct through language through reflection on experience. Language is the primary means by which we understand anything, but at the same time, language is also the primary means by which we falsify reality for ourselves and for others. So for Confucius, in similarity with the other religious traditions to which I have passed over in dialogue, the disciplined used of language as a means of apprehending truth without falsification and communicating truth is of utmost social and moral importance. Communal relationships between human beings absolutely require such discipline. For before a father can fulfill his filial responsibilities as a father, he must know what the meaning of the word "father" is. Before a son or daughter can fulfill their filial responsibilities to their parents, they must know what being a "son" or "daughter" means. Knowing what the filial obligations owed to a ruler are is absolutely required before a ruler can bring order to the state.

Thus the Superior Human Being uses words carefully and clearly, with as much univocal meaning as possible, without equivocation, so that when he or she speaks there is no ambiguity or misunderstanding about what is meant or intended. Social relationships are all too often broken because of unintended verbal misunderstandings. Furthermore, relationships between communities and states depend on linguistic clarity. The chaos of war has often originated in verbal misunderstandings.

"The doctrine of the mean" points to Confucius' teaching about how human beings should live in accordance with the *dao.* The Superior Human Being does nothing to access by ceaselessly seeking the proper balance between extremes in every communal situation while taking action accordingly. But unlike Philosophical Daoism, which counseled withdrawal from the rough-and-tumble of social and political interaction, Confucius sought to live in harmonious balance between *yin* and *yang through communal engagement* with the realities demanded by social and political obligations in the creation of a state that would help human beings live together peacefully and harmoniously.

Finally, the Superior Human Being practices "culture," sometimes called "the arts of peace." "To practice culture" may sound a bit odd to Western ears. But it helps to keep in mind what the word *wen* or "culture" means. Confucius believed that there are specific kinds of human creativity found nowhere else in nature that point to what all human beings share in common as individual reflections of the *dao*. He called this common reality *ren*, "humanity." *Wen* or "culture" is the objective expression that publically reveals *ren*, which constitutes us as "human": art, literature, philosophical reflection, calligraphy, technology, the "sciences." Study of culture and the practice of culture reveal what is unique about human nature and thereby makes us more humane. Thus, Superior Human Beings, through study and practice of culture, become, in the words of *The Book of Mencius* (or Mengzi), "sagely within and kingly without."[10] Accordingly, Superior Human Beings should not only study art, music, history, literature, philosophy, politics, technology, ethics, and poetry. Superior Persons should play an instrument or sing; make history; write their own poetry, short stories, or novels; be socially engaged with the rough-and-tumble of political realities; and be involved in the creative processes of technological innovation as they live their lives guided by the ethical principles of the "doctrine of the mean."

Obviously, Confucius' Way is not the mystical Way of the Philosophical Daoism, but the Way of social engagement with the hard realities of the political and ethical necessities required in constructing human community. I am not the first one to notice this, because the Chinese seemed to have viewed both traditions through the filter of China's classical worldview. As a Way of inner experience and withdrawal from the issues of statecraft in order to follow the natural ebbs and flows of nature, the Chinese typically view Philosophical Daoism as a *yin* Way of life. But as a Way of social engagement with the hard realities of communal life, Confucius' teachings were typically regarded as a *yang* Way of life. So the Chinese people, guided by their good sense, tried to live at the harmonious balancing point between

10. Chan, *A Sourcebook in Chinese Philosophy*, 67. Mengzi lived in the fourth century BCE. His interpretation of the meaning of the sayings of Confucius collected in the *Analects* became the foundation of the "orthodox" tradition of Confucian teaching and practice from the beginning of the Han Dynasty in the fourth century until the establishment of Mao Tse Tung's Marxist-Communist regime in 1948.

Philosophical Daoism and Confucius' teachings. For there are times when even politicians need to withdraw from their obligations and go into the country, "to get back to nature," so to speak, in order to return later to the obligations of social engagement refreshed and renewed. But *remaining* in a life of detached harmonious interaction with nature makes one's life irrelevant for life in community. Daoist hermits were not known for their engagement with politics. So most Chinese people took their worldview to heart and tried to combine Confucian and Daoist teachings in a harmonious balance—which is the core of pluralism of traditional Chinese religious tradition and practice.

## RETURNING

Certainly, the collective traditions of Confucianism and Philosophical Daoism are incredibly pluralistic and thereby incredibly complex. In this, Chinese religious traditions mirror non-Chinese traditions of faith and practice. Yet several themes emerge in Confucius' teachings and Philosophical Daoism to which Christians should pay serious theological attention.

First, learning to become human, according to Confucius, is a life-long process. The *Analects* is full of discourses on learning. Studying involves not just thinking and reflection, but foundationally, observation and listening. Learning must be supplemented with critical reflection on the meaning of what one has learned to be fruitful, meaning applicable to the ever changing issues that need to be resolved in creating harmonious communal life. While Confucius himself never claimed to be a Superior Human Being or Sage, he was absolutely committed to teaching others to become "sagely within and kingly without." So the overall scholarly tradition of Confucian tradition focuses on leading all persons to the Way (*dao*), the cosmic energy pattern overflowing and inflowing within all things and events at every moment of space-time. We can know the Way by learning, by scholarship, meaning knowledge of the arts that reveal the common human nature shared by all particular human beings everywhere at all times and in all places. Studying and learning the arts reveals that all human beings are utterly interconnected and interdependent, a notion very much in common with Western traditions of liberal arts education as well as contemporary natural science.

Of course, study and learning play important roles in Christian theological reflection, particularly after the early Christian movement gradually spread from its origins in Galilee and Judea in the first century throughout the Mediterranean world, where writers like St. Paul and the early Church fathers and mothers had no choice but to be in dialogue with Greek learning. Learning was given a jump-start as Greek philosophy and science entered Christian Europe in the thirteenth century, preserved in Arabic translations of Greek and Latin texts retranslated into Greek and Latin.

Today, "culture" includes not only the "liberal arts" like history, philosophy, languages, or literature, but also the "social sciences" like political science and economics, as well as the natural sciences along with study of and dialogue with the world's religions. I have always thought that the Confucian tradition "invented" what Western institutions of higher education now refer to as the "liberal arts." In the catalogues of any Western university or college one will find a paragraph about the value of liberal arts education. They all essentially affirm the same values that Confucian tradition means by the practice of "culture."

But for Christian tradition, the problem today is that theological engagement remains an elitist enterprise engaged in by professional theologians and a few pastors in local congregations who Sunday after Sunday try to relate their theological reflections to the life experiences of their congregations, who in turn have little interest in engaging in theological reflection for themselves because they are generally too busy with the daily chores of their lives. Furthermore, theological reflection too often remains isolated from other intellectual disciplines and the study and practice of theology is often locked in isolation within the specific ecclesiastical traditions of Christianity, in spite of the ecumenical movement. Particularly in many conservative and all fundamentalist Christian denominations, theological reflection is practiced as a prophylactic barrier to protect "faithful Christians" from contamination by what they either fear or dislike.

Certainly, Confucian tradition was an elitist tradition in China even as learning was, and remains, valued by the Chinese people generally. But Confucius' notion that the practice of "culture" reveals our common humanity rings true. All Christians, not just the theological elites, need to practice "faith seeking understanding." A major part of the practice of Christian faith requires the practice of "culture." Ordinary Christians should not allow theological elites to do their theological reflection for them, as Luther argued five hundred years ago, but should be engaged with the 2000-year history of Christian theology as they undertake the practice theological reflection for themselves. This means theological education—from pre-school to adult education—is foundational to the structure of Christian existence. This is so because authentic Christian faith is about engaging the truth in whatever religious or cultural dress it wears and following it no matter where it leads.

Second, living in harmony with the *dao* as portrayed in Philosophical Daoism has always been of interest to me. Seeking that point of balance between extremes seems both practical and wise. Not that I have always managed to remain in harmonious balance between extremes. Contrary to the Confucian and Daoist assumption that human nature is good, Christian tradition asserts a rather pessimistic view of human nature to which I subscribe because it reflects my own experience. While there exists a plurality of understandings about the nature of human sinfulness, the Lutheran tradition usually claims that sin is separation from God, nature, and other human beings generated by human egoism. Sin is clinging to ourselves as permanent selves, around which we try to make existence conform to our wills and desires, as if we were the center of the universe looking in rather than being an interdependent part of the universe. Ontologically, sin is part of our nature as human beings, the evolutionary origin of which evolutionary biology now refers to as "the survival of the fittest," not in disobedience of God by humanity's primal ancestors in the Garden of Eden. Immoral activity is not sin, therefore, but the result of sin. Thus human beings are *simul iustus et peccator,* meaning "at once justified and sinner," according to standard Lutheran theology. In other words, human nature is both good and sinful; human nature is not simply evil, which does not mean that there have not existed human beings whose actions have not generated unspeakable suffering to other human beings and to the environment.

Still there is something about the notion of living in harmonious balance with the forces of *yin* and *yang* that rings true. This can be illustrated by a positive and negative example: (1) the anthropic principle in contemporary physics; and (2) the metaphysical dualism assumed by most Western philosophy and traditional Christian theological reflection.

In the past twenty years, our understanding of physics and biology has noted a peculiar specialness to our universe, a specialness with regard to the existence of intelligent life. According to the "anthropic principle," the laws of Nature have particular constants associated with them, for example, the gravitational constant, the speed of light, the electrical charge, the mass of an electron, and Planck's constant from quantum mechanics. Some of these constants are derived from physical laws (the speed of light, for example, comes from Maxwell's equations). However, for most, their values are arbitrary. The laws would still operate if the constants had different values, although the resulting interactions would be radically different. Examples include:

- *The gravitational constant*: determines the strength of gravity. If it were lower, stars would have insufficient pressure to overcome the Coulomb barrier to start thermonuclear fusion (i.e. stars would not shine). If it were higher, stars would burn too fast and use up fuel before carbon-based life had a chance to evolve.

- *The strong nuclear force*: the strong force holds particles together in the nuclei of atoms. If it were weaker than it is, multi-proton particles would not hold together and hydrogen would be the only element in the Universe. If it were stronger than it is, all elements lighter than iron would be rare. Also radioactive decay would be less, which would increase the temperature of the Earth's core.

- *The electromagnetic force*: couples electrons to nuclei. If it were weaker, no electrons could be held in orbit. If it were stronger, electrons could not bond with other atoms. Either way, there would be no molecules.

All the above constants are critical to the formation of the basic building blocks of life. And, the range of possible values of all of these constants is very narrow, only about 1 to 5 percent for the combination of constants.

So the universe seems "fine tuned" for the possibility of life. For example, Stephen Hawking notes that had the rate of expansion of the universe one second after the Big Bang been smaller by even one part in a hundred thousand million million million, the universe would have recollapsed into itself shortly after it began expanding from its initial singularity.[11] The observed values of the physical constants seem balanced or finely tuned to permit the formation of commonly found matter and subsequently the emergence of life. A slight increase in the strong nuclear force would have prevented the nuclear fusion necessary to convert hydrogen to helium in the early universe. Water and the long-lived stable stars essential for the emergence of life as we know it would thereby not exist. More generally, small changes in the relative strengths of the four fundamental forces (the strong and weak nuclear forces, the electromagnetic force, and gravity) would have greatly affected the universe's age, structure, and capacity for life. It seems that from a physical standpoint, the universe exists at the

11. Hawking, *A Brief History of Time*, 291.

mid-point of balance in the ratios between the four physical forces since the first moments after the Big Bang. Increase or decrease the values of any of the four fundamental forces, everything devolves into chaos. Balance seems physically required for the existence of any universe having life in all its complex forms.

Of course, the anthropic principle is not an argument for the validity Philosophical Daoism's doctrine of *yin* and *yang*, just as it not an argument for the existence of God, as some Christian theologians have concluded.[12] Still, Daoist perception that life can only creatively flourish at the balanced cusp between polar forces seems congruent with contemporary scientific cosmology. Life lived at the extremes is not only self destructive, but communally and environmentally destructive. This is so because, from the perspective of the anthropic principle *and* philosophical Daoism, life exists on the cusp between too much or too little.

Accordingly, Christian faith and practice has much to learn from both Philosophical Daoism as well as contemporary physics and evolutionary biology about how we should live in balanced harmony with nature. Christian stewardship of the Earth requires that Christians oppose over-zealous, free-market, capitalist exploitation that threatens the survival of all life forms on Planet Earth as it destroys for profit the exquisite balances in nature that supports life itself. Living in harmony with nature, rather than exploiting nature, is an absolute necessity for survival on Planet Earth. Dialogue with Philosophical Daoism constitutes an important addition to Christian environmental engagement and activism.

There is also a tendency in Western culture generally, and Christian theological reflection specifically, to define oneself by what one is against. We live in a world where choices must be made, it is too often claimed, between that which we think reflects God's will and that which does not. According to conservative denominations of Christian tradition, gay sexuality and gay marriage are always wrong. Practicing birth control is against the teachings of Roman Catholicism *and* the will of God. God commands that we never eat pork or any other "unclean animal" and that we follow all the dietary rules and the rules of cleanness, if one is an Orthodox Jew or Muslim. Faithful persons practicing non-Christian religious traditions need to be converted to the one true religion, usually defined as one's own version of Christian tradition, if they are to be "saved" ("saved" from *what* is not usually very clear). The theory of evolution should not be taught in

12. See, for example, Dyson, *Origins of Life.*

public schools because it is leaves God out in its explanation of the origins of life. Secularism versus Christian faith; atheism versus Christian faith; and the list goes on. All of this is based on the duality of "them versus us," "us" meaning our particular Christian or non-Christian community and "them" meaning all religious or secular communities other than our own.

This sort of theological imperialism reflects the dualist assumptions of Western cultures since René Descartes. The world is generally split up into systems of "them" and "us" dualities, which always generates conflict, and often times, warfare between "them" and "us." Again, examples abound: democracy versus socialism; American "exceptionalism" (which is never defined precisely) that asserts the superiority of the United States over non-American nations; nowadays, enemies like terrorists, usually Muslims, must be defeated before they attack the United States again; liberals and progressives, usually associated with the Democratic Party, versus a deeply conservative Republican Party in an antagonism so strong that at present Democrats and Republicans cannot work together to resolve the political, economic, and social issues plaguing the United States. Similar dualisms creating conflict between communities too numerous to mention occur internationally.

What Christians can learn from Philosophical Daoism is that living in the extremes of either/or dualism is very dangerous and self-destructive, as well as communally and environmentally destructive. In fact, Philosophical Daoism's teaching that life guided by *wu-wei* is not all that different from the Synoptic Gospel's portrayal of what the historical Jesus taught his disciples about living in harmony with God's will, in contrast to the cultural values of his day.[13] Examples abound:

> You have heard that it was said, "An eye for an eye and a tooth for a tooth." But I say to you, do not resist an evildoer. But if anyone strikes you on the right cheek, turn the other also. (Matt 6:38)

> You have heard that it was said, "You shall love your neighbor and hate your enemy." But I say to you, love your enemies and pray for those who persecute you." (Matt 6:41)

> Therefore, I tell you, do not worry about your life, what you will eat and what you will drink, or about your body, or what you will wear. Is not life more than food, the body more than clothing? Look at the birds of the air; they neither sow nor reap nor gather into barns, yet your heavenly Father feeds them. Are you not of

13. See Borg, *Jesus*, 131–36.

more value than they? And can any of you by worrying add a
single hour to your span of life? (Matt 7:25–27)

Those who find their life will lose it, and those who lose their life
for my sake will find it. (Matt 10:39)

In other words, what the Synoptic Gospels, St. Paul, St. Augustine,
and Luther described as grace surrounds every living thing and event in
the universe like an ocean. We are not on the outside of our lives looking
in; there is nothing to achieve by clinging to either side of a *yin* and *yang*
dualism. Clinging to anything—self, another human being, a particular
religious tradition, a system of moral legalism, an idea or image of God,
or a particular viewpoint about the historical Jesus as the Christ—achieves
nothing. Absolutely nothing. If the Synoptic Gospels, Paul's Epistles, and
Luther are to be believed we are all floating in an ocean of grace. All we
have to do, all we can do, is let go and allow God's grace to take us where
it takes us.

# 7

# Wrestling with God

*Judaism*

## PASSING OVER

MY FAVORITE TEXT IN the Torah is the story of Jacob's wrestling match with God at the River Jabbok:

> Jacob was left alone; and a man wrestled with him until daybreak. When the man saw that he did not prevail against Jacob, he struck him on the hip socket; and Jacob's hip was put out of joint as he wrestled with him. Then he said, "Let me go, for the day is breaking," But Jacob said, "I will not let you go until you bless me." So he said to him, "What is your name?" And he said, "Jacob." Then the man said, "You shall no longer be called Jacob, but Israel, for you have striven with God and with humans, and have prevailed. Then Jacob asked him, "Please tell me your name." But he said, "Why is it that you ask my name?" And there he blessed him. So Jacob called the place Penuel, saying, "For I have seen God face to face, and yet my life is preserved. The sun rose upon him as he passed Penuel, limping because of his hip. (Gen 32:24–31)

Thus did Jacob the wrestler become Israel: "He who wrestles with God" and survives and spends the remainder of his life walking with a limp.

I have long thought that the story of Jacob's combat with God at the River Jabbok is a paradigm for the journey of faith for Jews, Christians, and Muslims.[1] According to the Prologue to the Gospel of John, there is never a time when God is not present in creation or in human history, so

---

1. See Ingram, *Wrestling with God.*

there is never a time when we are not encountering God, even if we are not conscious of the encounter. But as Israelite and later Jewish experience has demonstrated for over 3000 years, consciousness of God's presence invariably initiates a struggle that can be bruising. In Christian experience, the life of faith is always a struggle that engenders what Luther called "theology of the cross" because faith calls us, like it called Abraham, to a journey that takes us beyond the safe conventionalities of cultural, social, and religious boundaries. Faith is God's way of starting a fight with us. A hip—or something else—will be thrown out of joint, and we will limp through the remainder of our lives. Yet like limping Jacob, we are not defeated even as our wrestling match with God always leaves us with scars.

The story of Jacob's encounter with God at the River Jabbok is a central paradigm for the Jewish community's wrestling match with God guided by the Torah, God's "instructions" given to the people of Israel through Moses on Mount Sinai. God's Torah "instructs" human beings about how to live justly and compassionately in community as well as in harmony with nature. But it's one thing to be chosen by God to live according to the Torah so as to be a "light to the nations," as the prophet Isaiah put it; its quite another thing to figure out *how* to live in accordance with the Torah's instructions. So in imitation of limping Jacob who became Israel, Jewish history is a never-ending wrestling match with God to figure out what the Torah means and how to implement it throughout the changing conditions of Jewish history. It is for this, according to the Exodus traditions, that Israel was "chosen": to wrestle with God through the study of Torah and Talmud as interpreted through the lenses of rabbinic opinion as one seeks to follow the "commandments" (*halakah*) that have defined Israelite and later Jewish communal life for over 3000 years.[2]

The struggle to be God's "Chosen People" has cost the Jewish people dearly, for no religious community has suffered as much persecution as have Jews simply for being faithful to their covenant with God. Most of this persecution has been either initiated or supported by Christians. Atrocities committed against the Jewish community by Christians have their origins in the anti-Judaism of the New Testament.[3] By the fourth century, the New

2. The following description of Judaism is based on the following works: Cohn-Sherbok, *Judaism*; Hilberg, *The Destruction of the European Jews*; Fleshner, "Jews and Christians through the Ages"; Scholem, *Major Trends in Jewish Mysticism*; Rosenberg, *The Concise Guide to Judaism*; Efron et al., *The Jews*; and Sachar, *The Course of Modern Jewish History*.

3. See Ruether, *Faith and Fratricide*.

Testament's anti-Judaism morphed into Christian anti-semiticism, the beginning of a sixteen-hundred-year history of persecution that is so violent that the survival of the Jewish community seems itself an argument for the existence of God. Not even the Shoah or "catastrophe" could extinguish Judaism's light to the nations.

To a degree not found in other world religions, time and place—that is, history—matters for Judaism. This concern for the religious meaning of historical events was translated into Christianity and Islam. Thus the Tanak's collective narratives concern ancient Israel's engagement with history, empires, and kingdoms: the Exodus from Egypt, the time of Israel's kings, the exile in Babylonia, the return, and later developments in the homeland.

Throughout the historical experience of Judaism, certain concepts have remained constant, even as they have undergone adaptation. Accordingly, Jews live bounded within yearly cycles that mandate the observance of Sabbaths and sacred occasions—the New Year (*Rosh Hashanah*) in the early fall, *Yom Kippur* (the Day of Atonement), the Feast of Tabernacles (*Sukkoth*), Passover (*Pesach*), and Pentecost (*Shavuot*). Another cycle of rituals govern the great occasions of life from birth to death and, for orthodox Jews particularly, diet and dress.

The foundational stories of the Jewish people are those of ancient Israel and Judah recounted in the Tanak, which Christians refer to as the Old Testament. The Tanak consists of three large sections: (1) the Torah, also known as the Five Books of Moses (Genesis, Exodus, Leviticus, Numbers, Deuteronomy), which is the centerpiece of the Sabbath worship services; (2) the Prophets; and 3) the Writings, a collection of books diverse in style, including Psalms, Proverbs, and Ecclesiastes. Several of the stories in these texts provide the foundational narratives for later Jewish tradition.

According to Genesis, after the creation of the Earth and humanity and the destruction of the great flood, a clan emerged headed by the patriarch Abraham. Genesis relates the story of Abraham's covenant with God, or Yahweh (transliterated from Hebrew as *yhwh*), and God's promise to make a nation of Abraham's descendants through his wife Sarah in the land of Canaan. One sign of that covenant was the circumcision of all males among Abraham's people. God repeated the promises of the covenant to Abraham's son Isaac and to his grandson Jacob. Jacob had twelve sons. At a time of famine in Canaan, Jacob's descendants relocated to Egypt, where one of Jacob's sons, Joseph, who had been sold into slavery to the Egyptians by his jealous brothers, had risen to a position of prominence. Thus, by the end of Genesis, the children of Abraham reside in Egypt.

The book of Exodus opens several generations later when a Pharaoh, who did not know Joseph, feared that the expanding population of the Hebrews—now called the Children of Israel or the Israelites, after Jacob whom God renamed "Israel"—would unite with Egypt's enemies. Pharaoh enslaved the Children of Israel, and then ordered the death of all male newborns. But the infant Moses survived and, as the text relates, was found by Pharaoh's daughter floating in a reed basket on the banks of the Nile River and raised as an Egyptian in the palace court. As an adult, Moses fled to Midian after killing an Egyptian who was beating an Israelite slave. While tending the flocks of his father-in-law, he had an encounter with God who spoke from a burning bush that was not consumed. God told him to return to Egypt and free his people. God identified God's identity as "I am that I am" and told Moses to tell the Israelites that "The LORD, the God of your fathers, the God of Abraham, the God of Isaac, and the God of Jacob, has sent me to you" (Exod 3:14–15).[4] God also called Aaron, Moses' elder brother, to assist him.

After this encounter Moses returned to Egypt to negotiate the release of the Israelites, initially asking that they be permitted to go into the wilderness for three days to worship Yahweh and later demanding their exodus from Egypt. To convince Pharaoh to release the Israelites, God sent ten plagues, but Pharaoh only relented at the last of the plagues, the death of the Egypt's first-born male children. As the angel of death carried out this last plague, the Israelites were "passed over." Nevertheless, even as the people departed Pharaoh's army pursued, and the miracle of the parting of the Reed Sea allowed the Israelites to cross out of Egypt into the Sinai as the waters returned to drown Pharaoh's pursuing chariots.

Having successfully escaped, the Hebrews journeyed to Mount Sinai. There Moses received a new revelation, a new covenant between God and the people—they agreed to worship God, and God gave them the Torah condensed into the Ten Commandments, by which they were to live. The people accepted the covenant with God in return for God's promise to prosper the people of Israel, but soon afterward turned their backs on the Covenant by violating one of its essential laws prohibiting idolatry. Because of this, it would be a generation before God would allow the people to move

4. The Hebrew in the phrase "I am who I am" can also be translated in the past or future tense: "I was who I was" or "I will be who I will be."

from the Sinai wilderness into their promised land, Canaan, now called Palestine or "Land of the Philistines." And as punishment for the people's apostasy Moses was not allowed to enter the Promised Land. When he died, leadership of the Israelites was passed to Joshua.

It is at this point that the concept of Israel as a nation begins to emerge. The story of the next centuries is told in terms of the struggle to remain loyal to the Yahweh, in contrast to the surrounding polytheistic cultures, the struggle to fend off conquest by various neighbors, and the development of royal and priestly leadership. Israel was divided into the twelve tribes named for Jacob's sons. Joshua assigned territory to each tribe, and a series of seers, judges, priests, and prophets emerged to guide the people according to their understandings of the Torah's requirements. These leaders dealt with a range of problems and provided some overall guidance to this confederation of tribes.

During this time, worship was centered at Shiloh, where the symbol of the Israelites' covenant with God, the Ark of the Covenant, was kept and worship of God through an animal sacrificial cult was maintained by the priests. The ark of the covenant was lost to the Philistines during the battle at Ebenezer. The Philistine victory led directly to the Israelite decision to create their own monarchy. Around 1000 the kingdom of Israel emerged, with Saul as its first king. Saul's reign was followed by David's (about 1000–962). He defeated the Philistines and, after capturing the hill city of Jerusalem from the Jebusites, brought the Ark back to Jerusalem and made it the religious and political center of Israel. David's son and successor, Solomon, built the first Jerusalem temple, and from this time forward Jerusalem would remain the holiest city in Judah and for later Judaism.

Solomon's son and successor, Rehoboam (934–917), could not hold the kingdom together, and in 931 it split into two: the northern kingdom, which was called Israel, and the southern kingdom known as Judah, named for the largest of its two tribes. Both kingdoms prospered for the next two centuries. But in 721 the Assyrian Empire conquered Israel. A century later, when Assyria was conquered by Babylonia, the Babylonians overran Judah, and, in 597 and again in 586, captured Jerusalem, destroyed the temple, and exiled its most important citizens to ghettos—the first ghettos in human history—in the city of Babylon.

How these narratives of Israelite origins and history came to be recorded in the Hebrew Bible remains somewhat a matter of conjecture. But biblical scholars hypothesize that, during the time of the two kingdoms, differing oral traditions were recorded that were later, during the Babylonian Exile, redacted into what became the written Torah—Genesis, Exodus, Leviticus, Numbers, and Deuteronomy. One hypothesis argues that the original sources used different names for God—one preferring the name *Elohim* ("god") in the account of events prior to the revelation to Moses at Sinai, the other calling the Israelite God *Yhwh*.

The reigns of David and Solomon and the two kingdoms were also a time in which independent religious voices, those of the prophets, would arise to challenge the rulers and the priests wherever they saw subversion of the Covenant to faithfully follow the Torah, particularly by politicians and priests. Among the prophets, the voices of three collected in the book of Isaiah—First Isaiah, a prophet who lived in the eighth century BCE and whose prophetic speeches are recorded in chapters 1–39, and Deutero-Isaiah, which is a collection of prophetic speeches dating from the sixth century BCE in chapters 40–66,[5] and Ezekiel (also sixth century) stand out as the first clear declarations of monotheism in the Tanakh based on their vision that in the future all nations would come to worship one God in Jerusalem. More prophets would continue to arise among the Judahites even after Babylonia fell in 539 BCE to Persia.

The Persian king, Cyrus the Great (585–529) permitted the Jews—those who so desired—to return to Jerusalem and in 515 a second temple was rebuilt and dedicated. Those who remained behind in the Persian Empire formed the beginnings of the Diaspora, meaning "dispersion." From then until today, the history of the Jewish people includes the various civilizations where Jews have lived both within the land of Israel and in the Diaspora communities that have flourished and disappeared over the centuries.

In 332, Alexander the Great (356–323) captured Jerusalem. Following Alexander's death, his empire split among his generals. Judea first became part of the Ptolemaic Kingdom based in Egypt, and then around the year 200 it came within the orbit of the Seleucid Kingdom, centered in Syria. After several decades, the Seleucids clashed with traditionalists in Jerusalem and Judea. The issue came to a head during the reign of the Seleucid king Antiochus IV, who ruled from 175–163. In his attempt to suppress Jewish dissent, Antiochus desecrated the temple and forbade the observance of the Sabbath, the study of the Torah, and the practice of circumcision. His

5. Chapters 55–66 are a collection of diverse prophetic speeches dating from a different period than Deutero-Isaiah. The identity of the prophet or prophets who produced this collection of speeches is unknown.

actions sparked a revolt led by a family known as the Maccabees. Their recapture of the temple and its rededication are commemorated annually in the Jewish winter festival of Hanukkah or "Festival of Lights." Eventually, the Maccabees and their heirs threw off Seleucid rule and established a new independent Jewish state in 142 known as the Hasmonean Dynasty. This state would remain independent until the Roman conquest in 63 BCE.

During this period of independence, a variety of groups emerged within the Jewish community. Prominent among them were the Sadducees and the Pharisees. The Sadducees argued against the authority of much of the oral tradition of interpreting the Torah, opting to keep control of interpretation in the hands of the priesthood. The Pharisees argued for a broader interpretation of the Torah, using the oral tradition and placing authority in the hands the leaders of local synagogues called rabbis or "teachers." They sought to adapt the Torah's demands to the changing realities of Jewish life. The Sadducees comprised the hereditary priesthood of the Jerusalem Temple, and the Pharisees were the leaders of local meeting places for the study of Torah and prayer. The Pharisaic party would come to dominate, eventually giving rise to the era of classical Judaism, led by the rabbis and the great sages of the Jewish people. The Pharisees became the center of Jewish life after the Romans destroyed the Second Temple in 70 CE and are the direct forebears of Rabbinic Judaism.

As noted, Judea's independence ended with the arrival of the Romans. The turmoil of Roman occupation and the establishment of a local puppet government created an environment in which a wide spectrum of Jewish groups emerged. Among these was the Qumran community (Dead Sea sect), which was forgotten until a library of their material was uncovered in the 1940s in a cave on the edge of the Dead Sea, where they had retreated to create their communal society. The Qumran community lived a separated life marked by discipline and hope for the arrival of a messianic figure who would free Israel from foreign oppression and initiate the Kingdom of God with Jerusalem at its capital. Scholars have argued for over half a century over the possible influence of the Qumran community on the early Jesus movement that that eventually evolved into Christianity.

Both the Qumran community and the Jesus movement were symbolic of unrest in Judea, caused not only by an oppressive Roman occupation, but also by offensive Roman policies that were contrary to Jewish law and practice. A revolt against Rome broke out in 66, and a Roman army under Vespasian was dispatched to quell it. Vespasian was called back to Rome to become Emperor and Jerusalem fell to his son, Titus, whose army sacked Jerusalem and destroyed the Second Temple in 70. But resistance would continue in Palestine for a few more years, most notably at the mountain fortress Masada, where, in 73, its defenders committed suicide prior to its capture.

Even prior to the Roman era, Diaspora Jewish communities thrived around the Mediterranean Basin. Possibly thousands of Jews resided in Alexandria during the first century. In direct response to the loss of the temple, Jochanan ben Zakkai, a Pharisee, created a new school to continue the Pharisaic tradition of Torah interpretation. The learned Pharisees, or rabbis, as they were now called gradually fixed the canon of books known as the Tanak by 90 CE. With the temple and its sacrificial cult destroyed along with the concomitant loss of the centrality of the priesthood, the rabbinic leadership and the synagogue emerged as the center of Jewish communal life, prayer, and study of Torah. The rabbis also fixed the liturgies for the various synagogue services.

Equally important, the rabbis carried on discussions of applications of the Torah for daily living. They began to write down their viewpoints in commentaries, and, at the beginning of the third century, an initial authoritative edition appeared known as the Mishnah (literally, "repetition"). The Mishnah contains the opinions of more than 100 Jewish scholars. It continues to guide Jewish religious praxis today.

In the next centuries the process of Torah interpretation continued with the Mishnah as its foundation. In Palestinian academies in Tiberias and Caesarea, rabbis produced another commentary called the Gemara ("completion"). By the year 400 their commentaries with the relevant parts of the Mishnah were redacted into the text known as the Jerusalem Talmud. However, setting the Mishnah in writing also allowed the Jewish community at Babylon, which had continued from the sixth century BCE, to establish rival academies and interpretations. Their commentaries, also called Gemara, were redacted, with the relevant sections of the Mishnah, into the Babylonian Talmud by 500. These two Talmuds record the commentaries of more than 2,000 teachers and cover numerous topics not mentioned in the Mishnah. The attempt to establish the authority of the Talmud would lead to the emergence of one group known as Kararites, who rejected the notion of oral Torah and many of the rules and rituals derived from it. The Kararites still survive as a small minority tradition within contemporary Judaism.

The opinions contained in the Talmud, Mishnah, and Gemara, and all subsequent commentaries and texts constitute *halacha* or law ("walk," "practice," or "rule"). At this point an important clarification needs to be made. Judaism is often described as a religion of practice (*praxis*). Although Jews have the sort of convictions that Christians understand as "theological," Judaism does not emphasize "belief," as many forms of Christianity do. Rather, to be a Jew means to live as a Jew. This means observing the Torah and other Jewish teachings in daily life because the Torah concerns all of life, not just what persons today often think of as the religious part of life. Nor should Christians, particularly Protestant Christians, think of observing the Torah as "works" or Judaism as a "religion of law." Judaism in all its forms is based on the conviction that God has chosen Israel and that Israel has agreed to live in accord with God's covenant. Or to appropriate common Christian terminology, Judaism combines grace (God's choosing of Israel) and response to God's grace expressed through living according to *halakah*. So to be a faithful Jew means acknowledging God's covenant with the community and ordering one's life in conformity to *halakah*, which concerns every imaginable aspect of life. By following *halakah*, observant Jews sanctify life from moment to moment. Jews *do not* experience *halakah* as a legalistic burden.

While the rabbis were debating the laws of the Mishnah and Talmud, they also adapted the Jewish calendar and its holidays. The *seder*, a ritual meal celebrating the Israelites' deliverance from Egypt, was developed for the celebration of Passover. The rabbis fixed the future calculation of the Jewish calendar, which had once required witnesses to the new moon in Jerusalem. This guaranteed that Jews wherever they lived could celebrate holy days at the same time and in the proper season. It should also be noted that in antiquity Jews in the Diaspora had added a second day to their celebration of festivals, a custom that developed out of concern that word of the new moon's appearance might not reach Diaspora Jewish communities in time for the celebration of Rosh Hashanah. This explains why some Jews today celebrate a single day of many festivals, as is done in the modern state of Israel and among some contemporary Diaspora Jewish communities.

With the emergence of Sabbath liturgies, festivals, and rituals for holidays and life's passages, an ever-growing corpus of *halacha*, a fixed calendar, and a synagogue for every community Judaism appeared ready to survive until God would send the Messiah and return the Jews to the land of Israel.

Indeed, from a contemporary perspective, the first generations of rabbis built the platform upon which Jewish history would henceforth develop.

Through the dispersion of the Jewish community (even prior to the Roman era), Jewish ideas found their way into other non-Jewish communities in unexpected places. Jews traveled westward around the Mediterranean Basin, and a flourishing community emerged on the Iberian Peninsula. Very distinctive Jewish communities, including the Beta Israel and the Lemba, developed south of Judea in Yemen, Ethiopia, and even in Zimbabwe. Jewish communities also sprang up in the East, in Mesopotamia, Afghanistan, and India, where the Bene Israel and Jews of Cochin would become integrated into Indian culture.

The dispersion of the Jewish community was frequently caused by persecution. Jews encountered difficulties from the Romans, where Jewish monotheism was in serious conflict with Roman state religion that required acknowledging the emperor of Rome as a god. Jews also found themselves increasingly under attack from Christians, especially as Christianity developed into a separate tradition followed primarily by Gentiles who interpreted Christianity as superseding Judaism. In the seventh and eighth centuries, Islam emerged as a new force sweeping over of the Arabian Desert and across North Africa, into Spain, and throughout the Middle East to Mesopotamia, Persia, and Central Asia. By the eighth century, the majority of the world's Jews resided in the lands of the Muslim Caliphate, where they were mostly tolerated as a protected people. In many places in the Muslim world Jewish culture and intellectual life flourished.

Spain was an extremely important center of medieval Jewish life. Jews prospered under the Muslim caliphate from the eighth through the eleventh centuries but were persecuted when, at the end of the eleventh century, the Almoravid Dynasty from Morocco extended its control into Spain. During the next centuries Spain would be dominated by the interests of competing Muslim factions and the reassertion of Christian hegemony. The re-establishment of Christian rule in Spain and Portugal eventually proved disastrous for Jews, who were banished by King Ferdinand in 1492 and again in 1497.

Spain was also the birthplace of Moses ben Maimon (1135–1204), better known as Maimonides, who fled his homeland during the Almohades persecution and eventually settled in Egypt. He became the author of a large code of Jewish law, the *Mishnah Torah*. He also articulated thirteen principles of Jewish belief that include affirming the oneness of God, the revelation of Torah, and belief in the coming of the Messiah. With his love of Greek philosophy, especially Aristotle, Maimonides, the author of the *Guide for the Perplexed*, stood in contrast to another Spanish teacher, Moses de Leon (1250–1305), who lived and worked in Granada. De Leon lifted Jewish mysticism to new heights generally known as Kabbalah. Kabbalah portrays the cosmos as an emanation of God through ten realms called *sephirot*. The last of these emanations, *malkuth*, is roughly equivalent to the mundane world. For the Kabbalist, the Torah is a pathway to the experience of unity with God. De Leon's work would find a capable interpreter in Isaac Luria (1534–1572). Later, in the eighteenth century, a separate branch of traditional Judaism—Hasidism—would also emphasize Judaism's mystical tradition.

In the Middle Ages Jews also spread north from Palestine into Europe, establishing communities in England, France, Italy, Germany, and Eastern Europe. Although these communities often attained a stable life as minorities in Christian lands, their history was punctuated by periods of discrimination, persecution, massacres, and expulsions. Christians often blamed Jews for the death of the historical Jesus. Over time, Christian anti-Jewish animus engendered restrictive legislation, such as forcing Jews to wear an identifying badge and other laws reflecting the assertion that Jews were inimical to Western Christendom because Jews kidnapped Christian children for secret rituals. In this atmosphere of mistrust and misunderstanding, Jews faced the continual threat of sudden outbreaks of violence.

Jews were expelled from England in 1290 and from France early in the next century. The expulsion from Spain in 1492 led to further expulsions from Sicily (1492–1493), Lithuania (1495), Germany (1510), Tunisia (1535), and Naples (1641). At around this same time the first of the European ghettos segregating Jews from Christians were established. The first ghetto in Europe was created in Venice in 1516. As a result of expulsion and persecution, many Jews moved to Poland, which became a major center of European Jewish life. A vital community also developed in Holland in the sixteenth century, the most religiously tolerant state in Western Europe. Though segregated from the larger community, the Jewish communities in these countries developed a rich culture.

The expulsion of Jews from Spain led many to find refuge in the Ottoman Empire, which at the time stretched from the Balkans across the Middle East and into North Africa as far as Algeria. Many Jews also moved into the newly discovered Americas. They first "New World" Jewish community was established in Recife, Brazil, during its brief occupation by the Dutch (1630–1654). This was followed by Jewish dispersions throughout the Americas to such places as the Dutch settlement on the island of Curaçao and to the North American colonies of New Amsterdam (later called New York) and Newport, Rhode Island.

There were only six synagogues in the United States at the time of its founding; but throughout the nineteenth century the number of Jewish communities was greatly increased through immigration, first by tens of thousands of German and central European Jews and then by hundreds of thousands of eastern European Jews. The Jews from Northern, Central, and Eastern Europe, known collectively as Ashkenazi, outnumbered the original community of American Sephardic Jews, who traced their heritage through Spain and Portugal.

Throughout the eighteenth century, Judaism remained largely rooted in the teachings and traditions based on the texts that had developed in Palestine and Babylonia in the early centuries of the first millennium CE. However, during the late eighteenth and early nineteenth centuries, Jewish life underwent some remarkable changes, the result of the liberal policies toward Jews that originated during the Enlightenment, particularly the separation of church and state. The French Revolution had emancipated the Jews, granting Jewish men civil rights as individuals and annulling all French anti-Jewish legislation, while demanding that Jews adapt to French culture in return. The Napoleonic wars carried these ideas to Jewish communities across Europe.

Today Jews respond to modernity by seeking ways to integrate and assimilate into the larger Gentile society while maintaining their Jewish identity. One response is the creation of Reform Judaism, a way of being Jewish that emphasizes what are understood as the eternal truths of the faith, as opposed to irrelevant ancient practices. Arguing that God's revelation is progressive, German Rabbi Abraham Geiger (1810–1874) began to introduce changes into his synagogue in Breslau. Many traditional practices were discarded, including a variety of dietary restrictions and traditional beliefs were modified in favor of emphasis on an "ethical monotheism." Reform Judaism caught on quickly in the United States, where Rabbi Isaac Mayer Wise (1819–1900) championed its cause.

Rabbi Geiger encountered strong opposition among the traditionalists in the Jewish world. Rabbi Samson Raphael Hirsch (1808–1888) of Frankfurt am Main led the forces that would affirm traditional, or as it would come to be eventually called, Orthodox Judaism. In the United States Isaac Leeser (1806–1868) championed the traditionalist position in opposition to Rabbi Wise.

Between Orthodox Judaism and Reform Judaism, a third alternative was proposed by Rabbi Zacharias Frankel (1801–1875). He recognized both the need to respond to the new consciousness of history and the Reform idea that Judaism needed to change with the times. However, he rejected the radical stripping of "outdated" ritual from the synagogue, especially Reform's willingness to jettison Hebrew as the language of prayer. He appreciated ritual as an expression of deeply felt realities. He therefore proposed a third way that has subsequently come to be known as Conservative Judaism, or in contemporary Israel, the Masorti movement.

Simultaneously, the Hasidic movement, from the Hebrew *hasadim* or "pious ones," began in Poland, the product of both the Kabbalistic writings of de Leon and Luria and the experiences of men like Israel ben Eliezer (1700–1760), known as the Baal Shem Tov, the Master of the Good Name (of God). Reportedly an unlearned man, the Baal Shem Tov was known as a healer, and as a teacher he called into being a community whose centers were built around men known for one or more charismatic traits, often as wonder-workers. Although perfectly observant in belief and practice, the Hassidim and their courts were often seen as competitors to rabbinical Judaism and the synagogue. Many branches of Hasidism developed as different leaders established Hasidic communities in the various cities and countries of Eastern Europe.

In the second half of the nineteenth century, Jews continued to win emancipation in various countries in Europe. For example, several German states emancipated their Jews, and, in 1871, when Germany became unified, German Jews achieved full emancipation. But even as Jewish integration into European civilization continued, reaction against Jewish life and culture did not disappear. What had once been a religiously based animus against the Jewish people evolved into racial anti-Semitism, hatred of the Jews rooted in the idea that they were a distinctive race that bore immutable, degenerate characteristics and whose members sought to undermine the foundations of Western civilization.

The culmination of nineteenth-century anti-Semitism was the infamous Dreyfus Affair in France. Meanwhile in tsarist Russia, a new wave of violence broke out against Jewish communities following the assassination of Tsar Alexander II in 1881. Waves of violence, known as pogroms, continued for into the 1940s.

The violence and forms of Jewish hatred in the nineteenth century provided the environment in which Zionism developed. In 1896, Hungarian-born Theodore Herzl (1860–1904) published his call for a Jewish nation, and the next year he founded the World Zionist Congress to plan for a future Jewish state. The rise of Zionism also called attention to the growing secularization of the Jewish community. Many of the early Zionists rejected religious praxis and belief, even as they saw Palestine as the historic homeland of the Jewish people and planned to create a Jewish state there.

The idea of creating a Jewish state in Palestine, at the time still part of the Ottoman Empire, divided Jewish leaders. However, early supporters began to purchase land and moved to Palestine. Zionism as an international political movement gained ground when, in 1917, Lord Arthur James Balfour (1848–1930), the British foreign secretary, wrote a letter to Lord Rothschild confirming the sympathy of His Majesty's Government for Zionist aspirations. Between 1900 and 1930, a quarter of a million Jews migrated to Palestine, which had been taken over by the British when the Ottoman Empire was dismantled at the end of World War I. Migration increased during the next decade in response to persecution by the Nazis.

The history of the Middle East would likely have been very different had it not been for the Holocaust, the paradigm of contemporary racial anti-Semitism. The Nazis murdered six million Jewish men, women, and children. Even before the full extent of the tragedy was known, world sympathy flowed to the survivors. Following a 1947 United Nations vote to partition Palestine into a Jewish State and an Arab State, events moved rapidly. In May 1948 the British ended their mandate over Palestine, and Jewish leaders proclaimed the new state of Israel. The concomitant Arab Palestinian state did not emerge.

Crucial to the development of Israel since its establishment has been the Law of Return. Originally passed in 1950, this law sought to solve the problem of Jewish persecution by granting every Jew residing anywhere in the world the right to migrate to Israel. As a result of this law, millions of Jews from communities around the world have moved to Israel during its brief history. They include Jews from historic communities in Arab countries, like Egypt and Yemen, who fled renewed anti-Jewish persecution following the establishment of the state of Israel, and approximately a million Jews from the countries of the former Soviet Union. Though a small minority of Orthodox Jews (Neturei Karta, Satmar Hasidism) continue to lobby against Israel, believing the state should not exist until the messiah comes, the world's Jews overwhelmingly support the existence of the Jewish state.

Modern Jewish religious life remains centered around the synagogue. In turn, synagogues are organized into national associations of synagogues and rabbis. Each of the major Jewish groups, Reform, Orthodox, Conservative, and the most recently formed Reconstructionist community, have national organizations in each country where they have multiple synagogues. Orthodoxy is divided by cultural traditions; German, eastern European, and Sephardic Jews retain a level of separation (World Sephardic Federation), and new forms of Orthodoxy have arisen around twentieth-century issues (Young Israel and Gush Emumim). The national associations also participate in umbrella organizations serving the whole Jewish community, such as the World Jewish Congress, and some have formed international cooperative fellowships that serve their own constituency worldwide, such as the World Union for Progressive Judaism.

As of this date, the world's two largest Jewish communities are in Israel and in the United States. At this time they comprise more than 80 percent of world Jewry. Of the 5.2 million U.S. Jews, about half are formally affiliated to a synagogue. Some 5.3 million Jews reside in Israel, where they make up more than three-fourths of the population. Large communities also continue in France (491,000), Argentina (185,000), Canada (374,000), and the United Kingdom (300,000).[6]

## RETURNING

About fifteen years ago unnamed persons threw railroad flares at Temple Beth El in Tacoma, Washington. The northern exterior of the temple was severely damaged in the resulting fire. The specific motives for this attack are still unclear, but they were undoubtedly part of the long history of anti-semitism. For the next two months, an organization of progressive Christian churches called the Associated Ministries of Pierce County, Washington gathered a group of socially engaged Christians from several mainline churches and Muslims from the Tacoma Islamic Center and surrounded Temple Beth El during the night for the next month to prevent

6. Sachar, *The Course of Modern Jewish History*.

further attacks. This protective circle did not end until the arrest of the five perpetrators by Pierce County Sheriff's Deputies.

Eva Fleischner writes that there are many scholars who maintain that the relationship between Christians and Jews is a history of increasing hostility and persecution that culminated in the Shoah. This is the view of one of the most important historians of Judaism, Raoul Hilberg, for whom anti-Jewish church laws passed from 306–1434 parallel Nazi legislation from 1935–1942.[7] Yet Fleishner does not believe that this portrayal, while accurate, captures the whole picture. There is absolutely no doubt that centuries of Christian teaching and preaching provided a foundation for the Nazi Genocide, and that the church was often indifferent or complicit in the Shoah. Yet not all of the two-thousand-year-long history of Jewish-Christian relations can be reduced to a story of hatred and persecution. Nor was the Shoah inevitable. Accordingly, Christians who pass over into Judaism and return need to keep several facts in mind.

- The anti-Jewish polemics in the four Gospels were directed toward the Judaism of the first and second centuries, as well as to the Greco-Roman world. This also applies to some of the sermons of the early church fathers, for example, John Chrysostom.

- In the sermons of popular preachers throughout the Middle Ages, there are passages that express respect and admiration for Jews, for example, for Jewish commitment to keeping the Sabbath, high Jewish moral standards, commitment to learning and education, and fidelity to their faith even when confronted by persecution.

- Even during times of great danger to the Jewish community, such as the First Crusade in 1096, there were Christians, often holding important political offices, who spoke out and tried to defend and protect Jews.

- While there were numerous times of conflict, there were also times and places where Jews and Christians lived side by side in peaceful dialogue. For example, the "Golden Age" in Spain (called Andalusia) lasted three hundred years. During this time, Jews and Christians occupied important positions in a Muslim society. It was in Andalusia that Arab and Jewish scholarship and Arabic translations of Greek

7. Fleischner, "Jews and Christians through the Ages," 43. Also see Hilberg, *The Destruction of European Jews*, 5

philosophical and scientific texts were retranslated into Greek and Latin, which in turn laid he foundations for the European Renaissance.

- Papal edicts supporting Jews did not necessarily affect popular beliefs or prevent pogroms. Accusations of blood libel or ritual murder continued to be made in spite of papal decrees that denounced such charges as baseless.[8]

- Despite the proliferation of anti-Jewish literature in patristic and medieval times, the Roman Catholic Church never issued a theological or dogmatic proclamation against Jews or Judaism. Nor are Jews mentioned in any of the Christian Creeds.

- Despite the tragic history of Christian anti-Judaism, this history does not of itself account for the Shoah. It also took nineteenth century racism and modern technology to make the Shoah a reality. Christian anti-Judaism was not the sufficient cause of the Shoah, but it was a necessary cause. Apart from Christian anti-Judaism, Hitler would not have had such a receptive audience for his ideology.

Even so, none of these factors played as central a role in making the Shoah possible as did negative Christian teaching about Jews and Judaism. In the words of feminist theologian Rosemary Radford Ruether, "the church must bear a substantial responsibility for the tragic history of the Jews in Christendom which was the foundation upon which political oppression and anti-Semitism and the Nazi use of it was erected."[9]

The problem is rooted in 2,000 years of Christian exclusivist teaching and practice known as "supersessionism."[10] So long as Christians insist that Christian faith and practice, or some version of it, is the single truth about God's relationship to the universe and to humanity, and therefore all who

8. The term "blood libel" refers to the accusation by Christians that Jews kidnapped and ritually murdered Christian children because the role of Jews in Jesus' crucifixion created in Jews a lust for innocent blood. Jews were accused of crucifying young boys all over Europe into the twentieth century.

9. Ruether, *Faith and Fratricide*, 184.

10. "Supersessionism" is a recent theological notion that is frequently used in contemporary Jewish-Christian dialogue to denote the ancient Christian theological claim that Christians have replaced, or "superceeded, Jews as God's Chosen People, who lost this standing because Jews failed to recognize the Historical Jesus as the Messiah. Accordingly, the Jewish Covenant with God is null and void and is replaced by the New Covenant with Christians. Supersessionism is rejected by most mainline Protestant Churches, as well as the Catholic Church since Vatican II.

disagree are wrong, Christians will relate to Judaism (and Islam and other non-Christian traditions) in destructive ways. This is the standard form of Christian theological exclusivism that, in a plurality of ways, asserts that faith in the historical Jesus as the Christ is the only means of "salvation." But in my opinion, liberal or "progressive" Christians need to shift from Christocentrism to theocentricism as they affirm a pluralist theological stance. Such a shift would require Christians to recognize that Jews (and Muslims) relate to the same God as Christians, but in different yet truthful ways.

Such a shift in no way weakens what distinguishes Christian tradition from non-Christian traditions: 2,000 years ago in the historical Jesus, human beings encountered God incarnated in the historical Jesus as the Christ and continue to encounter God through the Holy Spirit. Certainly not all that God is, but nevertheless God. So in Christian interaction with Judaism, the most pressing problem is that all Christians, in a pluralism of ways, follow St. Paul in asserting that all who have faith in, that is, trust the historical Jesus as the Christ of faith are free from the demands of Jewish *halakah*. Christians, particularly mainline Protestant Christians, think that legal systems like *halakah* are something that may be necessary for human community, but all legal systems are a burden separating human beings from one other and from God. The mainline Protestant Christian point is that human beings are justified by grace through faith, not by obedience to legal standards or belief in doctrines.

But for Jews, *halakah* is not burdensome but joyful. Obedience to *halakah* binds Jews into community with one other and with God. It gives profound meaning to Jewish life. So what might appear on the outside to Christians as liberation from a legalistic religious system appears to Jewish experience as a loss of meaningful existence. But St. Paul, who was a first-century Diaspora Israelite, did not teach that there was inherent value in *not* observing Torah. For him, observing or not observing *halakah* was a matter of secondary importance for those in the Gentile Christian communities he founded. They were free to adopt either practice. Furthermore, since observant Jews did not, and still do not, press their way of life on Gentiles, Jewish commitment to observing *halakah* poses no theological problems for Christian acceptance of Judaism's way of following Torah.

But of course, this matter is not as simple as I have described. There exist Jews who find *halakah* traditions oppressive, and there are forms of Judaism that that greatly amplify *halakah* tradition. But my point is not that Christians need approve one tradition of Judaism over another. My point is

Christians can and should appreciate and learn from the plurality of Jewish discussions about the role of *halakah* observance in the Jewish community without negatively judging the value of Jewish legal traditions according to Christian theological assumptions.

This is so because in point of historical fact, law and ethics have always played an important role in Christian communities. The biblical roots of Christian ethics originate in the prophetic traditions of the Tanak. The teachings and life of the historical Jesus, himself Torah-observant, were particularly grounded in the prophetic traditions of ancient Israel and Judah. Accordingly, Christian faithfulness to the historical Jesus as the Christ requires adopting the ethical principles in the Tanak.

Accordingly, for Jesus and St. Paul the real problem is not so much "law" as "legalism." The historical fact is that Christians have often fallen into legalism from which St. Paul tried to free gentiles in the churches he either founded or visited. Yet despite the historical Jesus and St. Paul, most Christian communities have adopted quite legalist forms of life posing as "Christian." Martin Luther was particularly focused on this point in his arguments with the sixteenth-century Roman Catholic sacramental system. Yet even in Lutheran traditions, relapses into the legalism are a constant problem.

So when it is a matter of affirming the centrality of the historical Jesus as the Christ of faith, Christians, particularly liberal or progressive Christians, are obligated to clarify the teachings of Jesus and the theology of St. Paul to those who conclude that being a Christian is reducible to whatever legal systems are taught in Christian communities. As followers of the historical Jesus and St. Paul, Christians should not fall back into the legalisms the historical Jesus and St. Paul so strongly opposed.

Nevertheless, Christian focus on the historical Jesus and St. Paul does not require condemning those who center their lives in the Torah. Jews have derived a rich wisdom from the wrestling match with God that is required of anyone following God's Torah, and Christians have much to learn from Judaism's wrestling with God. So the direction that Christians need to follow in dialogue with Judaism does not entail abandonment of the centrality of the historical Jesus as the Christ of faith. That is, while the historical Jesus as the Christ is the center of Christian faith, this does not imply condemnation of those who live their lives out of other centers. But this understanding is threatened when Christians turn the historical Jesus into divine being who was not fully human, that is, as God appearing in human form. The Nicene Creed specifically speaks against this christology because it holds firmly to the full humanity of the historical Jesus. Christian recognition of God's presence in the historical Jesus does not contradict his humanity. Nor does it diminish his humanity.

But many conservative and all fundamentalist Christians, in contradiction to the New Testament and the Creeds, treat the historical Jesus as metaphysically different from all human beings. While accepting the creedal affirmations that Jesus had a fully human mind, nature, and will they also incoherently claim that the "person" of Jesus was "divine." In other words, Jesus' "self" was "God's self" rather than a "human self" in whom God was fully present. Furthermore, the Roman Catholic and the Orthodox Churches spoke of Jesus humanity as "impersonal," thereby losing the real depth and meaning of the Incarnation.

As a Progressive Christian, I side with the creeds in their insistence on the full humanity of the historical Jesus. But I also affirm that the historical Jesus is the Christ of faith because God was "in" Jesus. But since God is "in" all things and events at every moment of space-time since the Big Bang, as the Prologue to the Gospel of John declares, God's presence in the historical Jesus does not make Jesus metaphysically different from other human beings. His difference from other human beings seems to be that he was utterly responsive to God's presence in his life. Consequently, as much as Christians emphasize the work of God in and through the historical Jesus, doing so does not entail belittling God's work in and through other people or religious traditions.

Historically, the traditional Christian understanding of Judaism has been read through the notion of two covenants with God. Traditional Christian exclusivist and inclusivist theology affirms that God not only made a covenant with the Jewish people, but also a new covenant with Christians that has replaced the old covenant because Jews rejected Christian portrayals of Jesus as the messiah. It was this view that lead to denying "salvation" to Jews and energized missionary efforts to convert Jews to Christianity. Often Jews were blamed for the crucifixion of the historical Jesus, when in point of historical fact Jews had very little to do with it; the Romans crucified Jesus. But the assertion of Jewish blame for Jesus' death led to pogroms and set the earliest precedents for the Shoah. Most of the major contemporary mainline branches of Christianity have repudiated this supersessionist view as well as the historical error that Jesus was crucified by first-century Judeans. The point is that now, at least among progressive Christians, the covenant between God and Israel is not replaced by God's incarnation in the historical Jesus as the Christ. Accordingly, Christianity and Judaism (and Islam) are best understood as sister traditions.

This being said, the millennia-long persecution of Jews by Christians leaves many Jews unable to trust Christians. Many Jews believe, with good reason, that very few contemporary Christians truly comprehend what the experience of the Shoah means to the global Jewish community. However focused Christians might be in never allowing anti-Judaism or anti-semitism a foothold in the church again, it remains problematic that Christians are worthy of Jewish trust. This lack of trust is one of the main factors that leads many Jews to dedication to secure their own state where all Jews are welcome. As a progressive Christian, I understand this desire, sympathize with it, and unequivocally support the existence of the State of Israel.

But here's my problem. Even at its best, the establishment of a Jewish state in Palestine could not have occurred without a terrible price paid by Palestinians for the sins of Europe and America. Furthermore, the mutual animosities engendered by the way in which the state of Israel was created has brought tremendous suffering and oppression to the Palestinians and neighboring Arab states that few foresaw—and which is contrary to the ethical stadards of the Torah and the prophetic tradition. Certainly, the Palestinians and neighboring Arab states are not innocent bystanders in the awful events that have occurred in Israel and Palestine. Even so, the Palestinians are the victims of European and American policies, and the injustices inflicted on them are often magnified by the decisions of Israel itself, the most glaring example being the opening of new Israeli settlements on Palestinian territory on the West Bank and other territory captured in the 1967 War. As a Progressive Christian, I oppose this form of Palestinian suppression.

I suppose that it might be argued that all this is a quite separate question from Christian dialogue with a sister Abrahamic tradition. But for many Jews the centrality of the Torah includes the centrality of God's gift of the land now known as Palestine to the Jewish people. It is therefore difficult for most Jews to distinguish criticism of the policies of the government of Israel from Christian attacks on Judaism. This problem becomes more intense because most Jews understand the recent history of Israel in ways that give extensive moral justification to the actions of Israel that oppress Palestinians that many Progressive Christians like me condemn. But to many Jewish ears, this criticism sounds biased and anti-Jewish.

Thus in much of my dialogue with Judaism regarding the State of Israel I am caught between two evils: (1) the evil of silence about the massive injustice done to Palestinians, much of it supported and even financed by the American government, and (2) the evil of heightening Jewish anxiety that Christian friends cannot be trusted, which in turns drives many Jews to more strident efforts to safeguard the State of Israel at still greater oppression of Palestinians. Even so, many progressive Jews are deeply concerned about extending justice and compassion to the Palestinian people because they believe that the most hopeful future for Israel lies in generosity to those who have paid such a high price for making the State of Israel a reality. The most appropriate role for Christians is to support this segment of the Jewish community.

# 8

# "That We May Know Each Other"

## *Islam*[1]

## PASSING OVER

WHEN AN AFRICAN AMERICAN imam named Siraj Wahaj served as the first Muslim "chaplain of the day" in the United States House of Representatives on June 25, 1991, he offered the following prayer, the first Muslim prayer in the history the Congress:

> In the name of god, Most gracious, Most merciful. Praise belongs to thee alone; O God, lord and creator of all the worlds. Praise belongs to Thee Who shaped us as and colored us in the wombs of our mothers; colored us black and white, brown, red, and yellow. Praise belongs to Thee who created us from males and females and made us into nations and tribes that we may know each other.[2]

Siraj Wahaj's prayer is a direct reference to one of the most cited verses of the Qur'an: "Do you not know, O people, that I have made you into tribes and nations that you may know each other."[3] Of course, "to know each other" is an important goal in the practice of interreligious dialogue

---

1. See the following works that serve as the foundations of this chapter. Murata and Chittik, *The Vision of Islam*; Hussain, *Oil and Water*; Schimmel, *Mystical Dimensions of Islam*; Esposito, *Islam: The Straight Path*; Esposito, *What Everyone Needs to Know about Islam*; and Craig and Speight, *The House of Islam*.

2. *American Muslim Council Report* (summer 1991), cited in Eck, *A New Religious America*, 32. Also see Ingram, "That We May Know Each Other."

3. Surah 49:13. All citations from the Qur'an are taken from the English translation of Yusuf Ali.

and requires breaching social, ethnic, gender, and religious boundaries. But Muslims often move on to cite further Qur'anic advice about religious pluralism: "If God had so willed, he would have made you a single people, but his plan is to test you in what he hath given you; so strive as in a race in all virtues."[4] According to Imam Wahaj and the vast majority of Muslims, Islam and pluralism go hand in hand when it comes to asserting the dignity of all human beings no matter what religious or secular label he or she wears. Of course, this interpretation of the Qur'an is rejected by minority radical communities within the House of Islam as well as by fundamentalist communities within Christian, Buddhist, Hindu, and Jewish tradition. Nor are the foundations of pluralism found only in the Qur'an. There exist important progressive Buddhist, Jewish, Hindu, and Christian traditions that support religious pluralism as well.

Yet for the vast majority of Americans and Western Europeans Islam is currently the most misunderstood, vilified, and stereotyped of all religious traditions. Part of the reason for this is Islamic-Christian animosity that goes back to the earliest years of the spread of Islam beyond Arabia, particularly into territories claimed by the Christian rulers of the Byzantine Empire, and, in Medieval times, to a series of Christian Crusades to wrest Jerusalem and surrounding Palestinian territory from Muslim control. The theological source of the conflicts between Christianity and Islam originate in the absolutist claims of both traditions to be the final revelation of God to humanity. Add to this history the displacement of thousands of Muslims from their homes in Palestine by the creation of the State of Israel and the radicalization of numerous Islamic groups that have appropriated the concept of *jihad* ("struggle") to justify horrendous acts of terrorism, a recent example of which is the destruction of the World Trade Center in New York by hijackers of a United Airlines and an American Airline passenger jets and the damage to the Pentagon by another captured airliner on September 11, 2001. Over three thousand innocent persons died in these acts of terrorism. Some of these persons were American Muslims. A further problem is that Islam's contemporary portrayal in most Western news media is profoundly inaccurate and stereotyped, which to be fair is the way Western print and television journalism portray most religious traditions and practices.

So more than any other religious tradition I taught during my work with university students, I had to spend more time dealing with inaccurate

---

4. Surah 5:51.

stereotypes about Islam. The same is true when I am invited to introduce Islam to adult education classes in local church communities.

In particular, I remember a three-week series at Messiah Lutheran Church in Auburn, Washington like it was yesterday. At the first session on Sunday morning, September 10, 2001, thirty-five people were gathered in the choir room. These Lutherans were interested in Islam because many of their neighbors and friends were Muslims and they wanted understand them. So I spent the first session discussing Mohammed's life and teachings as described in Islam's Holy Book, the Qur'an.

On the morning of September 11, as I was eating breakfast, I watched television coverage of the attacks on the two World Trade Center towers and the Pentagon and listened to reports of how a group of passengers fought with hijackers on another airliner heading for the White House and crashed the plane into a field in Pennsylvania killing everyone on board. When I arrived at Messiah Lutheran the following Sunday morning for my second session, I was met by the pastor in the church's parking lot as I pulled in. He informed me that the class would be meeting in the sanctuary, where about three hundred members were waiting for me. So I just walked down the center isle and said, "I see you have some questions," and spent the rest of my time at Messiah Lutheran dealing with whatever questions people had about Islam. What struck me most was how these folks thought that the terrorism of September 11 did not represent Islam and that it was now urgent for them to accurately understand their Muslim brothers and sisters. Sometimes, perhaps more often than not, people sitting in pews in local congregations are wiser than their denominational leaders or elected politicians. What follows is a descriptive account of Islam that I offered to the good people at Messiah Lutheran Church.

Four defining elements of Islamic teaching and practice make it unique among the world's religions. Of course, all religious traditions are "unique." For example, the affirmation that all religious traditions eventually lead faithful persons to union with Brahman is deeply ingredient in much Hindu faith and practice. The Four Noble Truths, non-self, impermanence and Awakening define Buddhist teaching and practice in all its plurality of expressions. Seeking to live in balanced harmony with the Dao is the starting point of both Daoist and Confucian traditions. Judaism's Covenant to wrestle with God by following the Torah defines Jewish faith and practice in all is expressions. The Incarnation—two-thousand years ago in the life, death, and resurrection of a Galilean peasant of Judean heritage, human beings met God—is the foundation of the diversity of Christian faith and practice.

But there are several aspects of Islam that define its uniqueness among the world's religions. First, Islam is the only world religion that defines itself as "religion." The verbal noun *islām* appears eight times in the Qur'an and is derived from the same Semitic root as the Hebrew *shalom* or "peace." "Peace" does not mean mere absence of conflict, but rather the "wholeness" or "integration" that persons experience when they live peacefully in community with one another and with nature. Thus "Islam" means "surrender" to God's will and intention that human beings live in peaceful harmony with one another and with the natural forces through which God creates and sustains all life. "Religion" or *dīn* is the practice of substituting one's will for oneself with God's will.

But it's one thing to say that we should surrender our will for ourselves to God's will for us and for the universe. It is quite another thing to specify *what* God's will is and *how* to surrender to it. Thus the Qur'an specifies a guide for surrendering to God's will called the "Five Pillars" that define Islamic faith and practice. These pillars represent Mohammad's own religious practice and provide a model against which all Muslims test and measure their Islam. They are: (1) the *shahāda* (the "declaration"); (2) daily prayers five times a day (*salāt*); (3) almsgiving (*zakat*); (4) fasting during Ramadan (*sawm*); and (5) undertaking a pilgrimage to Mecca (*hajj*) at least once in one's lifetime. The Pillars of Islam (*arkān al-Islam*) are also referred to as *arkān al-dīn*, ("pillars of religion") and constitute the five basic practices obligatory for all believers. The *Qur'an* also presents them as a framework for worship and a visible sign identifying all "Muslims," meaning "she or he who surrenders to God's will."

The "Declaration" is the closest thing to what Christians mean by the word "creed": "*ašhadu lāilāha illā llā Allāh wa-muhammad rasūl 'allāh*," or "I bear witness that there is no God but God and Mohammad is God's messenger." The Declaration is the foundation for all other beliefs and practices in Islam. It is recited daily, particularly during times of personal and communal prayer

Ritual prayers (*salāt*) must be performed five times a day: in the morning upon arising, noon, mid-afternoon, evening, and before retiring to sleep. The purpose of prayer is to focus the mind on God as one ritually expresses his or her intention to surrender completely to God's will. All forms of Islamic prayer embody this intention. While Salāt is compulsory, it is also flexible depending on circumstances. For example, surgeons cannot and should not stop a medical procedure at noon to pray, or fire fighters should not refrain from putting out fires during times of prayer. For as the Qur'an states, God does not require of a person what that person cannot or should not do; it is the intention of the heart that matters most to God. Daly prayers are recited in Arabic either publically at a mosque or "prayer place" or privately and consist mostly of verses from the Qur'an. As places of communal prayer, any and all types of buildings dedicated to prayer are referred to as a mosque. Although the primary purpose of a mosque is to serve as a place of prayer, it is also as a place to meet and study and often serves as a community center.

Zakāt or "almsgiving" is offering a fixed portion of one's accumulated wealth to help the poor or needy. It is considered a religious obligation, as opposed to voluntary charity, that the well off owe to the needy because their wealth is seen as a "trust from God's bounty." The Qur'an also suggests that a Muslim give even more as an act of voluntary alms-giving. Those who surrender to God are responsible for the welfare of all Muslims and non-Muslims living in an Islamic community.

Fasting (ṣawm) from food and drink, sex, and the normal activities of daily life must be performed from dawn to dusk particularly during the month of Ramadhan, the most sacred time in the Islamic calendar of Holy Days. For forty days Muslims are to focus attention on the life and teachings of Mohammed as recorded in the Qur'an and in the record of his life and practice as recorded in the Sunna, a collection of stories about what Mohammed did and said apart from the Qur'an's revelations. The purpose of fasting is to focus completely on God while expressing gratitude for God's will, as exemplified by the Prophet, while seeking atonement for past lapses and offering alms to the needy. But Fasting is not obligatory for the ill or young infants, for whom it would constitute an undue burden. Again, God does not require of a person that which that person cannot or should not do.

The required pilgrimage to Mecca takes place during the Islamic month of Dhu al-Hijjah. Once in one's lifetime every able-bodied Muslim should make the pilgrimage to Mecca. Mecca is the place of origins not only of the Arab people, but is also is the birthplace of Mohammad and Islam. The entire cycle of pilgrimage rituals takes about ten days to fulfill. But again, the Qur'an specifies that if circumstances make it impossible to fulfill the pilgrimage obligation, another Muslim can go in one's place so that one can make an interior pilgrimage of the heart. Again God does not require of a person that which that person cannot or should not do.

The second unique element of Islam is that more is historically known about the "founder" of Islam and his specific teachings than the "founder" of any other world religion. The following is a brief biographical sketch of the important details of Mohammad's life upon which most Muslim and non-Muslim scholars agree.

Mohammad was probably born in Mecca in 570, but this is not certain. It *is* certain that he died on June 8, 632, as reckoned by the Western calendar. His family was the Banu Hāshim of the Quraysh tribe. Because he was born after the death of his father, he became the ward of his grandfather, Abd al-Muttalib. At an early age, he experienced a visitation by what he believed to be two angels. This was the first of several experiences that led him to begin his search for God. At the same time he was employed by a widow named Khadijah to take trading caravans north into Syria. On these journeys he met Christians and Jews, and on one occasion a Christian monk named Bahira, who believed that Mohammad might be the messiah. When he returned to Mecca he married Khadijah, who was fifteen years his senior, and fathered two sons, both of whom died shortly after birth, and four daughters.

Because of his earlier religious experiences and his interactions with Christians and Jews, Mohammad grew more and more dissatisfied with the polytheistic traditions of most Arab tribes and the worship of their ancestor deities at a shrine in Mecca called the Ka'ba, which Arabs believed was the origin spot of the Arab people and Muslims believe was founded by Abraham as a place of worship. So he went with increasing frequency into isolation in a cave on the outskirts of Mecca on Mount Hira in order to resolve the truth about God lying behind the incredible pluralism of Arab polytheism. On one of these occasions he experienced the presence of the angel Gabriel who ordered Mohammad to "recite" three times (the word "Qur'an" means "Recitation"). At first Mohammad resisted, but then recited the first of many subsequent revelations: "Recite in the name of your Lord who is the most generous, who teaches by the pen, teaches man what he knows and what he knows not"—the opening words of Surah or "chapter" 96.

After he returned to Mecca he experienced further revelations and began preaching that the deity he encountered through the mediation of the angel Gabriel was the only God there is and that all the other deities that the Arab people revered were illusions. But his call to monotheism made him enemies, particularly among his tribe, who became wealthy through their control of the center of Arab polytheism, the Ka'ba. Because of his revelations, Mohammad believed with absolute clarity that if God is God, there can be no other: there cannot be a "Christian God" or a "Jewish God" or the "gods" of Arab polytheism. It therefore followed that the idolatry at Mecca was deeply wrong and must be abolished. In other words, Islam began as a monotheistic reformation among the Arab people. In this sense the whole of Islam is a footnote to this simple observation: there is only one God, Allah or "the God," and all creation is derived from Allah.

Accordingly, Mohammad proclaimed, all human beings should live in community ('umma) through surrender to God's will that human beings live together in justice and harmony under the sovereignty of the only God there is. This message was violently opposed by the Meccans. But Khadijah and his cousin, Ali, converted to Mohammad's teaching, followed by the first non-family convert, Abū Bakr, who after Muhammed's death in 632 became the first "successor" or khalīfa. Because of pressure against Mohammad and his "companions," some of which was quite violent, Mohammad was invited to Yathrib to settle a conflict between two rival factions. His journey to Yathrib, now called Madina, in the year 622 is regarded by Muslims as the center of Islamic history. That is, Muslims date theologically important historical events "before the "flight" or hijrah "or "after the hijrah." At Medīna the content of his revelations differed from the ones he received in Mecca. The Meccan revelations in the Qur'an are essentially calls to monotheism, while the revelations he received in Medina focused on working out the social, political, and ethical implications of monotheism.

But the conflict Mohammad experienced in Mecca spilled over to Medina in the form of military conflict, and finally at the Battle of Badr, Mohammad's forces decisively defeated Mecca. Mohammad then returned to Mecca, destroyed the idols in the Ka'ba, and made the city the religious center of his movement. But he went back to Medina, which became the political center of Islam. Ten years later, in 632 or the tenth year of the hijrah, he died on his final pilgrimage journey to Mecca. His body was taken back to Medina, where he lies buried in the Mosque of this city.

While Muslims and the Qur'an assert that Mohammad is the "seal of the prophets," Muslims do not believe this invalidates the prophets of the Tanak or the historical Jesus, whom Muslims view as a prophet rather than a redeemer or incarnation of God. God has continually revealed his will to human beings since the time of Adam—regarded as a prophet in the Qur'an—to Abraham; Moses; the eighth-, seventh-, and sixth-century Israelite and Judahite prophets; and Jesus. But Jews, Muslims assert, failed to live according to the Hebrew prophet's call for justice and compassion in community, and Christians incorrectly transformed the historical Jesus into a deity through the doctrines of the Incarnation and the Trinity, which the Qur'an regards as *shirk* or "idolatry." "Idolatry" is reducing God to that which cannot be God and submitting to these illusions accordingly. But finally, the Qur'an states, God has revealed his will to human beings in a simplified form that is clearly understandable. So there can no longer exist any excuse for not surrendering to God, who judges all human beings accordingly.

Therefore, Muslims believe, Islam is not the only true religion. As "Peoples of a Book," God's will has been revealed to Jews and Christians through the Tanak and the New Testament. But Islam is the "perfection of religion" and Mohammad is the "Seal of the Prophets,'" meaning that after Muhummad's death there are no further revelations and no further prophets. They are not needed because now human beings know what surrendering to God's will means and how to do it.

The third unique element of Islamic tradition is that more is historically known about the origins of the Qur'an ("Recitations") than the scriptures of any other world religion. There is little historical doubt among Muslim and non-Muslim scholars that the Qur'an in fact is a record of Mohammad's religious experience and teachings.

The fourth unique element of Islam is that the Qur'an is the only scripture in the world's religions that defines itself as "scripture": "This is the Book; In it is guidance sure, without doubt, to those who fear Allah" (surah 2:1). The Quran is comprised of 114 chapters (*surahs*) of unequal length that are classified either as Meccan or Medinan depending upon the place and time of revelation. Chapters are ordered by their length, with the longest chapter as the second surah and the shortest chapter as the last surah. The first surah is called "the Opening" and is only a few verses in length. Muslims believe that each surah in the Qur'an was verbally revealed through angel Jabrīl (Gabriel) from God to Mohammad gradually over a period of approximately twenty-three years beginning in 610 when Mohammad was 40, and concluding in 632, the year of his death. The Qur'an is also unique among the world's religious scriptures because of its explicit prohibition of racism and its assertion of equality between men and women: the biological differences between men and women *are not* to be used as male justification for oppressing women. Of course, this does not mean that Muslim women have never been oppressed by Muslims men. But whenever this has happened, it is contrary to the explicit commands of the Qur'an. Furthermore, the historical fact is that women in Mohammad's community experienced more freedom than women anywhere else in the seventh century.

Shortly after Mohammad's death, the Qur'an was compiled into a single book by order of the first Caliph, Abū Bakr. At the suggestion of Abū Bakr's future successor, Umar Hafsa, Mohammad's widow and Umar's daughter were entrusted with that Quranic text. When the future third Caliph, Uthman, began noticing slight differences in pronunciation of the Qur'anic Arabic by those whose dialect was not that of the Quraish, he sought Hafsa's permission to use her text and commissioned a committee to produce a standard copy of the Qur'an to which were added diacritical marks to ensure correct pronunciation. This pronunciation was set as the standard Arabic dialect, the Quraish dialect, now known as Fus'ha (Modern Standard Arabic). Five of these original Qur'ans were sent to the major Muslim cities of the era, with Uthman keeping one for his own use in Madina. Any variations to this standardized text were invalidated and ordered destroyed. This process of formalization is known as the "Uthmanic Recension." The present form of the Qur'an's text is accepted by most scholars as the original version compiled by Abū Bakr. Muslims believe that the words in the Qur'an are the actual words of God given to Mohammad as transmitted by the Angel Gabriel. While similar to Christian fundamentalist exegesis of the Bible, according to which the words of the Bible are the actual words of God, mainline Roman Catholic and Protestant tradition understands the historical Jesus as the Christ as the Word of God through which one should figure out the meaning of words in the biblical texts.

It is, course, one thing to affirm that human beings ought to surrender to the only God that exists; it is quite another thing to spell out how to interpret God's will and surrender to it within the ever-changing historical situations of personal and communal life. Jews face a similar problem in figuring out what living by the Torah means in the ever-shifting conditions of Judaism's long history. Of course, for Muslims one tests and measures one's surrender to God by the Qur'an and the Prophet's example as recorded in the Qur'an and the collection of stories about Mohammad's life and sayings called the Sunna ('Tradition of the Prophet").

But the Qur'an and the Sunna do not always helpfully refer to new or shifting cultural and historical circumstances. Accordingly, a Muslim also tests and measures his or her Islam by the *Shari'a* (Literally, "the path leading to the watering place"), or "law" or "jurisprudence." Shari'a is Islamic law formelated by traditional Islamic legal scholarship, which most Muslim groups adhere to. For Muslims, Shari'a is the expression of God's will and constitutes a system of duties that are incumbent upon every Muslim.

Islamic law covers all aspects of life, from matters of state, like governance and foreign relations, to issues of daily living. The Qur'an defines *hudud* ("forbidden acts") as the punishments for five specific crimes: unlawful intercourse, false accusation of unlawful intercourse, consumption of alcohol, theft, and highway robbery. There are also laws against apostasy, although Muslim scholars disagree about its proper punishment. The Qur'an and Sunna also contain laws of inheritance, marriage, and restitution for injuries and murder, as well as rules for fasting, charity, and prayer. However, these prescriptions and prohibitions may be broad, so that their application in practice varies from Muslim society to Muslim society. Islamic scholars (known as *ulama*) have elaborated systems of legal decisions on the basis of these rules called "*fiqh*" that function as legal precedents.

*Fiqh* or "jurisprudence" has evolved, and continues to evolve, to prevent innovation or alteration in the original religion, known as *bid'ah*. The method Islamic jurists use to derive rulings is known as *usul al-fiqh*, meaning "legal theory" or "principles of jurisprudence." According to Islamic legal theory, law has four foundations, which are given precedence in this order: the Qur'an, the Sunna (the practice of Mohammad), the consensus of the Muslim jurists (*ijma*), and analogical reasoning (*qiyas*). For early Islamic jurists, theory was less important than pragmatic application of the law. In the ninth century, the jurist al-Shafi'i provided a theoretical basis for Islamic law by codifying its principles.

There exist several traditions within the House of Islam that illustrate the pluralism in Islamic teaching and practice. The numerically largest tradition of Islam is Sunni Islam, which takes its name from the collection of stories about the life and sayings of the Prophet recorded in the *Sunna* or "tradition." Sunni Muslims comprise approximately seventy-five percent of all Muslims. In Arabic, *al-Sunnah* literally means "tradition" or "path." The Qur'an plus the stories of Mohammad's life and decisions recorded in the *Sunna* (in individual "stories" called *hadith*) are the primary foundations of Sunni practice. This is so because examples of how Mohammad lived his life in surrender to God's will are normative for figuring out how all Muslims should surrender to God's will in similar circumstances. The classical Muslim jurist al-Shifi'i (d. 820) emphasized the importance of the Sunna in determining the specific laws comprising the Shari'a. For Sunni Muslims, Sunna is also understood as crucial to guiding interpretation of the Qur'an. Sunni Muslims also recognize four schools of law: Hanafi, Maliki, Shifi'i, and Hanbali. All four schools accept the validity of the others and a Muslim may choose any school he or she finds agreeable. A very conservative form of Islamic jurisprudence is the Wahhabi movement, which is the foundation of the legal system in Saudi Arabia.

Shi'a Islam constitutes roughly twenty-five percent of practicing Muslims. Shi'a Muslims focus on the political and religious leadership of imams or "teachers" who regard Ali ibn Abu Talib, Mohammad's cousin and son-in-law, as the true successor to Mohammad. That is, while Sunni Muslims believe Ali was the Fourth Caliph, Shi'a Muslims believe Ali was the first Imam ("Teacher"). Accordingly, Shi'a Muslims replaced the Sunni caliphs with a tradition of Imams whose authority is by right of divine appointment and who hold absolute authority in matters of religious practice and law.[5] That is, since Shi'a Muslims believe Ali was Mohammad's true successor, future Imans are appointed by divine will. Thus even though Shi'a Islam shares most of the traditions and practices of Sunni Islam, they differ about the validity of specific collections of *hadith*. Shi'a Muslims also believe that at the time of Allah's final judgment of the world, Allah will send a final Iman to lead all oppressed Muslims in a final *jihad* or struggle against the forces of all domination systems oppressive to Islam.

Running through both Sunni Islam and Shi'a Islam is the mysticism of Sufi Islam. Sufism is a mystical approach to Islam by which seekers not only attempt to fully surrender to God's will as specified in the Qur'an and the teachings of the Prophet, but to achieve experiential unity or *tawhid* with God's will by suppressing through self-discipline their own individual wills; in such a state of awareness, the Sufi's will *becomes* Allah's will so that he or she can make a perfect act of submission to God. Thus Sufis engage in disciplined forms of contemplative prayer like *dikr*, or meditating on God's will as they recite the Ninety-nine Beautiful Names of God in the Qur'an, as a means of maintaining awareness of God's presence in the midst of their

5. In both Sunni and Shi'a Islam, all teachers of Islam and the leaders of local mosques are addressed as imans, but in Shi'a Islam an "the Iman" is the spiritual and political leaders of an Islamic community.

daily activities, much like the Hindu practice of *japam*. By this means, the Sufi's daily activities are transformed into ceaseless acts of surrender to God will. Generally, Sufis regard Mohammad as the model of their particular practice of Islam.

In order to illustrate the pluralism of Islam, mention must be made of Ahmadiyya, an Islamic reformist movement founded in British India near the end of the nineteenth century. Ahmadiyya Islam was founded by Mirza Ghulam Ahmad (1835–1908), who claimed to have fulfilled the prophecies about the appearance of a world reformer at the end times as predicted in Judaism, Christianity, and Islam and who would bring about the final triumph of Islam. He thus claimed that he was the Mujaddid (divine reformer), the promised Messiah of Judaism and Christianity, and the Madhi awaited by Muslims. The adherents of the Ahmadiyya movement are referred to as Ahmadis or Ahmadi Muslims.

Ahmadi Islam emphasizes the belief that Islam is the final dispensation for humanity revealed to Mohammad as recorded in the Qur'an along with restoring Islam to what they believe is its true form, which they believe has been lost through the centuries. Accordingly, Ahmadis view themselves as leading the revival and peaceful propagation of Islam and are particularly known for their nonviolent interpretation of *jihad* or "struggle." Ahmadiyya Muslims contend that God sent Ahmad, like Jesus, to end religious wars, condemn bloodshed, and reinstitute morality, justice and peace. They believe that he divested Islam of fanatical beliefs and practices by championing what is, in their view, Islam's true and essential nonviolence.

Ahmad founded the movement on March, 23 1889, and called it the *Ahmadiyya Mualim Jama'at* ("Ahmadiyya community"). Ahmadis consider themselves Muslims and claim to practice Islam in its pristine form; however, some Ahmadiyya-specific beliefs have been interpreted as contrary to mainstream Islamic thought since the movement's birth. Many mainstream Muslims do not consider Ahmadis to be Muslims, citing in particular the Ahmadiyya teaching about the death and return of Jesus at God's final judgment, the Ahmadiyya concept of *jihad* as nonviolent struggle against injustice, and its recognition of the founders of all the world's religions as "prophets." Ahmadis are also very much engaged in interreligious dialogue. In several Islamic countries today, Ahmadis remain marginalized and often oppressed by the majority Sunni and Shi's communities, which has led many Ahmadis to emigrate to England, Canada, and the United States. Saudi Arabia has also banned Ahmadis from the *hajj*.

Finally, I would like to conclude this section by noting the importance of Islam in the history of the natural sciences and the role of Muslim scholars in the preservation of the texts of Greek "natural philosophy" in Arabic translations, which were then retranslated by Muslim and Jewish scholars living in Damascus and Andalusia Spain into Greek and Latin from the seventh to the twelfth centuries. These translations in turn laid the foundations for the European Renaissance.[6]

From an Islamic standpoint, the study of nature is linked to the concept of *tawhid*, meaning the "unity" or "oneness" of God. Islamic scholars understood natural processes as expressions of God's will. That is, by being what they are "naturally," animals, plants, the orbits of the stars, the moon, and the sun, as well as the physiological processes of the human body, are paradigms of surrender to God's will. Accordingly, by observing natural processes and rationally understanding them, human beings can learn how they too should surrender to God's will. While the natural order surrenders to God "naturally," human beings must learn to surrender to God's will through reflection and through observation of nature. In other words, the Qur'an's approach to nature is what Christian theology refers to as "natural theology."[7] The pursuit of scientific knowledge is viewed in the Qur'an as a compilation of signs pointing to the Divine. It was with this understanding that the pursuit of science flourished in Islamic civilizations, specifically during the eighth to sixteenth centuries.

The Qur'an and the Sunna's encouragement of empirical study of nature inspired medieval Muslim scholars, in particular Alhazen (965–1037), to develop scientific methods. Advances made by medieval Muslim astronomers, geographers, and mathematicians were often motivated by problems encountered in the Qur'an, such as Al-Khwarizmi's (780–850) development of algebra in order to resolve Islamic inheritance laws along with developments in astronomy, geography, spherical geometry, and spherical trigonometry in order to determine the direction of the *qibla* (the pointer to Mecca in a mosque), the specific times of daily prayer, and setting the important dates in the Islamic calendar.

The use of dissection in Islamic medicine during the twelfth and thirteenth centuries was influenced by the work of the Al-Ghazali, who encouraged the study of anatomy and used dissection as a method of gaining knowledge of human physiology. This culminated in the work of Ibn

6. For a fuller discussion, see Dallal, "Science, Medicine, and Technology."
7. See surahs 13:1–18 and 27:59–62.

al-Nafis (1213–1288), who discovered the body's pulmonary circulation system in 1242 and used his discovery as evidence for the Islamic doctrine of bodily resurrection.

Finally, Fakhr al-Din al-Razi (1149–1209) discussed cosmology. He criticized the Aristotelian notion of the earth's centrality within the universe and explored the possibility of the existence of multiverses in the context of his commentary on the Qur'an, based on the verse, "All praise belongs to God, Lord of the Worlds" (surah 1:2).

## Returning

While the challenge of Islam to Christian understanding of the historical Jesus as the Christ is similar to Judaism's challenge, it is also quite different. Mohammed was aware of Christianity and Judaism because he had encountered Jewish and Christian Arab tribes and had met Christians and Jews as he led trade caravans throughout the Middle East. The Christian doctrine of the Trinity seemed to him to undermine the unity of God by its deification of a historical human being. For Mohammad, Jesus was an extraordinary prophet, and in his view had Christians not transformed Jesus into a deity by reducing God to a human being, which is *shirk* or idolatry, there would have been no necessity for God to send corrective revelations to Mohammad. Muslims believe this is the most fundamental difference between Islam and Christianity.

About fifteen years ago I taught an introductory course in Islam in which half my students were from Saudi Arabia, four from Kuwait, a few Iranian Shi'a students who had relocated to Sweden, a Bosnian Muslim refugee, and two Kurdish Muslims whose families had immigrated to Seattle. These students enrolled in this particular course because my university required all students to take two courses in religious studies. It must have seemed strange taking a course in Islam from a Lutheran historian of religions. But on the last day of the class, when my Muslim students stayed behind to chat, one of my Kuwaiti students smiled and said, "Not bad for an Infidel." I regard this as the best student evaluation I ever received.

During one of our discussion sessions, one of my fundamentalist Christian students declared, "Jesus is Lord." The Muslim students kindly tried to ask this student and me for an explanation they could comprehend, because from their point of view, "There is no God but God." I tried to let my Christian, mostly Lutheran, students lead the way in the discussion, but finally I was asked to offer my opinion. So I said, for me, the Incarnation is not a declaration that "the historical Jesus is God," but that *in* the historical Jesus Christians think they encounter God within the rough-and-tumble of an actual human being's life, death, and resurrection. Jesus is not God, and he did not declare himself to be God. But incarnated in this Jewish peasant's life two thousand years ago, human beings apprehended something of what God is like.

My Muslim students agreed that my interpretation of the historical Jesus' relation to God was not an example of *shirk*, but nevertheless, of course, they were unable to recognize Jesus as nothing other than an extraordinary human being God called to be a prophet that Christians have misunderstood for two thousand years. This opinion reflects the traditional Islamic claim that Muslims have built on Christian tradition and have moved beyond it. And in point of fact, if being a Christian entailed treating the historical Jesus as if he were God, I would have to agree with the Qur'an's insistence on the absolute unity of God—a point that perhaps distances me from most Christians. As I agree with Jews that Jesus does not meet their expectations regarding the Messiah, I also agree with Muslims that some traditional Christological formulations seriously threaten the unity and uniqueness of the One whom the historical Jesus addressed as "Abba" or "Father."

Conservative and fundamentalist Christians often engage in comparisons between the historical Jesus and Mohammad as a demonstration of Christian superiority. But these comparisons do not do justice to either the historical Jesus or to Mohammad. First, although Muslims regard Mohammad as the "seal of the prophets," they do not assert that he is an incarnation of God or that his person is the final revelation of God. Even Mohammad is not regarded as the center of history. Simply stated, through Mohammad, God revealed God's will for humanity that was set down in written form in the Qur'an. As John Cobb notes, "The supernaturalism that is too often part of Christian description of Jesus pertains, in Islam, not to Mohammad but to the Qur'an."[8] For me, as a Lutheran progressive Christian, I can accept neither Christian supernaturalism nor Islamic supernaturalism. Authentic Islam does not depend any more on treating the Qur'an as supernatural than authentic Christianity depends on treating the Bible or Jesus as supernatural. But of course, most Muslims and conservative Christians would disagree with me on both points.

8. Cobb, "Theological Response," 197.

Still, the differences in the role of the historical Jesus in Christian faith and experience and the role of Mohammad in Muslim faith and experience does, in fact, point to an incommensurable difference between Christianity and Islam. The historical Jesus is portrayed as a Jewish mystic, prophet, and teacher of wisdom and nonviolence in the synoptic Gospels.[9] Certainly, his teachings were grounded in the eighth-, seventh-, and sixth-century Israelite and Judahite prophets. It is as a prophet and teacher of wisdom and nonviolence that Jesus is the source of ideals that are seen to test and measure all human communities, while at the same time proclaiming a commonwealth or kingdom of God that is both a present reality when one feeds the poor and nonviolently resists unjust domination systems that oppress human beings *and* a future fulfillment that "comes like a thief in the night."

Following Mohammad as the "seal of the prophets" means creating just communities even if this means taking up arms in defense of those who are oppressed. The history of Christian theology includes reflection about relating the nonviolent wisdom teachings of Jesus to the hard realities of political life and military force. Islamic justification of "minor *jihad* or "struggle" against those judged to be oppressors cannot be associated with the nonviolent teachings of Jesus regarding compassion toward one's neighbors and enemies or his assertion that God's character is best described as "love."[10] This is not to say, of course, that Christians have consistently practiced nonviolence. And in point of fact, Islamic notions of "minor *jihad*" are in many ways similar to Christian "just war" theory.

Still, at least for progressive Christians, the historical Jesus as the Christ is central to faith and practice. For me this means commitment to living in the tension between the ideals taught by the historical Jesus and the demands of a sinful world. Which means I find the revelation of God's purposes for the world—for the universe as such—in the historical Jesus as the nonviolent paradigm of authentic Christian faith and practice.

9. See Borg, *Jesus*, chaps. 4–5.

10. The Qur'an discusses two forms of *jihad*. The "major *jihad*" is the life-long "struggle" against one's ego and self-interest that separates one from God and the human community, while the "minor *jihad*" is the struggle one should engage in defense of persons being unjustly oppressed by a political or economic system or because of their religion. Forced conversions or persecution of non-Muslims is not permitted by the Qur'an because "there cannot be compulsion in religion." See surah 2:56. It needs o be noted that this is in stark contract with the history of Christian attempts to compel persons either into Christianity or into some "orthodox" version of Christianity.

Still, I must admit that the struggle to relate Jesus as an example of nonviolent struggle for justice is extremely perplexing and highly ambiguous. For those who regard Mohammad as the greatest of the prophets, the relation between teaching and actuality is much closer than in Christian experience. Progressive Christians can understand and appreciate the link between Mohammad as a prophet and his role as a political and military leader, even if a progressive Lutheran Christian like me cannot share it.

Nevertheless, Jesus' teachings give very little direct guidance for ordering the human community, so there is much to be admired in the Qur'an and the Sunna in this regard. Yet Christians have for two thousand years believed that it was necessary to Christianize all aspects of their lives in community. But is it consistent with what we historically know about Jesus' teachings and practice to think of his message as dealing only with certain dimensions of life, leaving business, the professions, government, and the military outside his focus of concern? The historical Jesus was certainly a religious *and* political revolutionary in the way he questioned the existing domination systems of his time, particularly those of Rome, by his proclamation that God's "kingdom" or "commonwealth" was "at hand," an everlasting community of justice and peace established by God, that would replace the domination systems of his time. Accordingly, most Western Christians have allowed secular thinkers and political systems to take over most of this territory, yet not without critique or criticism.

My point is that, with the exception of Muslim communities in Western Europe, Canada, and the United States, Islam has retained a character that was once that of Christian tradition as well. But the contemporary secular world strongly objects to any religious institution that claims all of life as its province. Many contemporary Christians also object, particularly progressive Christians. I also object to laws that are imposed when a nation is organized on Islamic principles or principles that claim to be Islamic but are not, for example laws oppressing women or not permitting women to obtain an education. Christian history is full of similar injustices carried out in the name of the historical Jesus as the Christ. The church has too often claimed too much authority, and its power corrupted it. For this reason, I agree with Luther. A Christian state is an illusion, for there is no such thing. Secularization has done much to rectify this history, but it too has brought losses.

Nevertheless, progressive Christianity—and progressive Judaism and Islam—has the potential to create a unified vision that can refocus service to God and the human and nonhuman community with which we share this planet in place of service to wealth and power. Islam too resists much that needs resisting. As one who is committed to living in the tensions brought into the world by the teachings and practice of the historical Jesus as the Christ of faith, I deeply respect those who follow other religious paths involved in social engagement against unjust systemic forms of economic, social, and military oppression. In conceptual, interior, and socially engaged dialogue with non-Christian ways of living in this world, I continue to be inspired to search for new ways of resistance to injustice within my own tradition. Finally, Christians should be grateful to Muslim and Jewish scholars for their contributions to not only the origins of the natural sciences, but for their continuing contributions to contemporary science–religion dialogue.

I shall conclude this chapter with an account of just how inspiring dialogue with Muslims can be. From 1966–1975 I was a member of the faculty in religious studies at Simpson College in Indianola, Iowa. This college was founded by Matthew Simpson, a Methodist pastor, bishop, and abolitionist, in 1861 at a time when Indianola was one of the northern terminals of the underground railway bringing slaves north to freedom before and during the Civil War. But during my tenure at Simpson, there were very few people of color living in town, other than those who were students at Simpson College.

One evening in 1973, a Muslim student called me to ask me if he could come to my home for advice about a research paper he was writing for my seminar on interreligious dialogue.

"Of course," I said to Abdul. As we sat in my living room discussing his thesis that Sufi mysticism, like Thomas Merton's " monastic dialogue," could provide a means by which Muslims might be able to engage in an interior dialogue with Christian mystical experience, Gail, my four-year-old daughter came in and sat on the couch next to Abdul. She had seen persons of color before, but for some reason she became very curious and stared at Abdul.

Abdul, who was from Egypt, smiled back and said, "*salam*, Little One."

Then she brushed her hand across Abdul's left cheek. "Daddy, why doesn't it come off?"

"Ask Abdul," I said.

When she did, Abdul replied, "Because this is the way God made me."

"Why did God do that"?

"Because God loves wondrous diversity."

So from an excellent undergraduate student and faithful Muslim, my daughter received her first lesson about the delusion of racism. For me, it was Islamic confirmation of the justice of Martin Luther King's fight against American racism that energized my own involvement in the Civil Rights Movement and protest against the war in Viet Nam. For as the creation theologies of Christianity, Judaism, and Islam affirm, we live in an interdependent universe. As God's creation, all human beings are brothers and sisters in spite of the religious labels we choose or choose not to wear. We should, therefore, as the Qur'an asserts, "strive as in a race" for peace and justice "so that we may know each other."

# 9

# Why *Are* There So Many Different Religions?

As I NOTED IN chapter 3, I have been haunted by a koan-like question since my undergraduate days: "If there is only one God, why are there so many different religions?" In Rinzai Zen Buddhist meditative practice, a koan is a kind of question that is incapable of resolution through use of reason and intellect. They are neither puzzles nor riddles, but unanswerable questions that are objects of meditative concentration, the purpose of which is to still the emotions, intellect, and rationalizations of everyday conventional engagement with the world so that the reality holding all things and events together can break into consciousness in a sudden or gradual flash of insight. As Paul Knitter writes, "Koans . . . are words that are used to show the inadequacy of words, thoughts, and images, and their purpose is to project students beyond all thoughts and images."[1] In similarity with the words of Christian mystical theology, they are words of "unsaying."[2]

According to Zen tradition, the reality holding everything together is "beyond name and form," yet is named "Emptying" (*śūñyatā*)—note the cognitive dissonance! In Christian tradition, the practice of contemplative prayer is in many ways similar to koan meditation, except that the reality holding everything together that is experienced beyond name and form is named "God." Note that both "Empting" and "God" are names for that which is literally beyond names, yet must be "named" in the conventional speech of those of us who have not achieved Awakening or experienced union with God, as well as by those who *have* experienced Awakening or union with God. Which means that persons experience conventionally through a religious tradition's practices what their philosophies or

1. Knitter, *Without Buddha, I Would not Be a Christian*, 63.
2. Sells, *The Mystical Languages of Unsaying*, 63.

theologies train them to expect to experience. So like a koan, "If there is only one God, why are their so many religions?" continues to be for me an object of both rational reflection and meditation.

Here's part of my problem, to which I referred in chapter 3. "Why questions" are not normally the business of historians of religions. We are trained to deal with descriptive "how questions," much like the natural scientists are concerned with describing the "how questions" that explain the origins and physical realities that account for the structures of the universe. "Why" the universe is as it is cannot be answered by means of scientific methods of investigation. The moment a scientist engages with a "why question," that scientist becomes a theologian or philosopher. Which does not mean that "why questions" are unimportant or that scientists should not engage them.

Similarly, the methodologies of historians of religion can only engage descriptive "how" and "what questions." For example, how do religious traditions and practices reflect the history and social structures of a particular community? How do the history and social structures of a community affect a religious tradition's historical development? What does evolutionary biology, particularly the neurosciences, tell us about the origins of religion and the physical foundations of religious experience? What are the similarities, if any, and the differences between the world's religious traditions? And the list goes on. But the methods of history of religions are as unsuitable for dealing with normative or "why questions" as rational reflection is for resolving a koan.

There exist other "why questions" the solutions to which cannot be found through the collective methodologies of history of religions. To which religious tradition *ought* persons commit? Do Buddhist teachings and practices accurately reflect the structures of existence? Do Christian or Jewish or Muslim or Hindu or Chinese traditions? Can any religious tradition be judged as "truer" than the rest? These sorts of normative questions require theological reflection "at the boundaries," or if one is a nontheist, philosophical reflection "at the boundaries" that join conventional ways of knowing with the language or "unsaying" employed by mystics in all the world's religious traditions.[3] Any solution also requires engagement in interreligious dialogue that also, in my opinion, requires dialogue with the natural sciences as a third partner.[4]

3. See Ingram, *Theological Reflections at the Boundaries*, chap. 1.
4. See Ingram, *Buddhist–Christian Dialogue in an Age of Science*, chaps. 1–2.

This is why I am *not* asserting that historians of religions should disengage from theological or philosophical "why questions." Scholars in my field should refuse to be limited by the Cartesian dualisms that balkanize academic disciplines into territories having no relationship other than being other. So in protest against this ghettoizing of fields of knowledge, I have consciously chosen to wear two methodological hats: that of historian of religions and that of Lutheran theologian informed by his work in history of religions coupled with his dialogue with the natural sciences." "How questions" and "why questions," descriptive questions and normative questions, are utterly interdependent.

So as a theological pluralist, I find myself in a Lutheran tradition of faith and practice that does not normally support theological pluralism. The tension lies between my Lutheran path and my perception that the universe in general and the reality I name God in particular is not capable of reduction to any theological, philosophical, scientific, or Christian system of belief or ideas. In reflection on this tension, I have received help from my Buddhist friend and colleague, Mark Unno. He writes:

> From within my own religious path, Shin Buddhism provides ways in which to enter this pedagogical circle ("dialogue") of theological complementarity. First, in the realm of form, of multiplicity and religious attachments, I am a foolish being blinded by attachments. Thus, in order to awaken beyond the limited horizon of my own religious perspective, I need to allow other perspectives to enter into and enrich my being. Second, from within the order of oneness, which is, as Shninran states, beyond "orthodox and heterodox," there is a point from which all theological perspectives are embraced. Emptiness is not emptiness until all is embraced; the ocean of light loses brilliance if it is divided.[5]

As a Lutheran theological pluralist, I can only agree. From within my own path, St. Paul's, Augustine's, and particularly Luther's understanding of God's grace provides me with a way to enter the dialogical circle of complementarity, namely: God's "ocean" of grace pouring over all human beings, indeed, all things and events at every moment of space-time. Yet in a world of multiplicity and religious divisions and attachments, I too am blinded by my particular attachments, commitments, and theological perspective, including my pluralist perspective. But I also know from what the historical Jesus taught concerning God's nature as love and God's passion for justice

5. Unno, "Contemparative Theology with a Difference," 267.

as an expression of love, I need to awaken beyond the limited horizon of my own theological perspective, indeed beyond the limits of Christian tradition itself. For the historical Jesus might have been a practicing first-century Jew, but he taught that God doesn't give a damn about "religions," but passionately cares very much about human beings and the rest of creation. God is not confined by or limited to human expectations, even Christian perspectives. So I need to allow non-Christian perspectives to enter into, enrich, and creatively transform my being as a Lutheran Christian. This is the case because from within the depth's of God's continuing creativity there exists, as Margarite Porete and John of the Cross experienced, what Shin Buddhists refer to as an "Ocean of Oneness" beyond orthodox and heterodox, a point at which all religious perspectives are embraced.

In other words, the reality Christians name God is not the only name to indicate what the word "God" means. Pluralism is ingredient within the human condition, which means that we cannot "understand" or signify what the words "God," "Allah," "Brahman," "Dao, or "Emptying" mean in terms of a single perspective or principle of intelligibility. Hindu, Buddhist, Chinese, Jewish, Muslim, and Christian names for the Sacred may symbolically point to whatever the Sacred is, but they never capture the "object" to which they symbolically point. For God, Brahman, Dao, and Emptying, and Allah are not "objects."

So when all is said and done, it's all about transcendence. This is of course, the most important lesson we learn from what interior dialogue between Christian and non-Christian mystical experience tells us about the focus of theological thought and reflection. As Tom Christenson writes:

> Some people suppose that talk about transcendence is talk about the super-natural. This is not the way I want to use the term. Something is transcendent if it goes beyond ourselves, for example if it calls us or demands something from us, or lures us on to a new level of seeing, understanding, or being.[6]

Then Christenson cites one of my favorite hymns in the Lutheran liturgical tradition that is based on the twenty-third Psalm: "Shepherd me, O God, beyond my wants, beyond my fears, from death into life." He notes that it is easy to understand a prayer to fulfill our wants or to avoid our fears. But how can we pray to move beyond our wants and fears? This is transcendence, when something that does not originate from our wants

6. Christenson, "The Oddest Word," 179

and fears captures us and stretches us beyond our wants and fears, perhaps even beyond our imagining. "Such an encounter can be the occasion of my growth, my conversion, my death and rebirth, my arrival as a new person."

A story or the practice of meditation or contemplative prayer can do this. So too can insights into the physical processes at play in the universe do this. Hindu experience of the numerous incarnations of Brahman can do this. Encountering the *dao* can do this. Wrestling with God's "instructions" in the Torah can do this. Experiencing Allah's *tawḥid* or "unity" can do this. Encountering God's incarnation in the historical Jesus as the Christ of faith can do this. Engaging in conceptual, socially engaged, and interior inter-religious dialogue can do this. Engaging in interreligious dialogue with the natural sciences can do this. The experience of transcendence has multiple particular forms, but each throws us, sometimes kicking and screaming, out of the conventional limits of our knowledge and linguistic constructs, into boundary constraints that expand our experiences into new possibilities never previously imagined or encountered.

So given the boundary constraints of human knowledge, can anything really be said? In an important sense, the answer is "yes," because a great deal has been said and written by Hindus, Daoists, Buddhists, Jews, Muslims, and Christians. Indeed, everything I have written in this book is an attempt to contribute to what has been said and what may be said. But can things be said about ultimate transcendence clearly and unequivocally? The lesson of the natural sciences and interreligious dialogue is "no." This is why as a Lutheran Christian process theologian I have come to understand that conceptual, socially engaged, interior, and science–religion dialogues are the proper forms of meaningful theological reflection in a culturally and religiously plural world that is always changing, always becoming.

So should religious persons remain conceptually silent? Perhaps the best answer is, "probably more than we do." When we do engage in dia-logical conversation, we should speak and write mindfully, as the world's mystical traditions inform us, aware of the temptations involved in trying not to speak or in speaking too much. Again, following the instruction of the sages, in speaking about things that reflect transcendence, we need to speak and write in an intentionally impaired language by using words that cannot be uttered, in language with a deliberately warped grammar of un-saying, words that always carry a warning: the words we speak or write are not final words.

But all of this being "unsaid," what *can* I say about my *koan?* What follows is definitely *not* written in a language of "unsaying," but in the language of a Lutheran historian of religions process theologian engaged in dialogically passing over and returning. As such, I can only speak for myself and hope others on their particular religious paths can find some assistance with their own faith journeys.

About six years ago I encountered my koan and a monotheistic solution in a book published by John Berthrong titled *The Divine Deli:*

> I not only accept the fact of religious pluralism, namely that God really did create all of the different religions with their fabulous diversity, but that, like all of creation, diversity is fundamentally good. However, this primordial fact of goodness does not mean that there are no problems with the world. All one has to do is look around to make the informed guess that not all is in line with the desire of a loving God.[7]

Bumping into Berthrong's book now seems to me like more evidence of grace. So I shall add my voice to defending the idea that monotheism filtered through the lenses of a pluralistic theology of religions provides an adequate answer to my koan: If there is only one God, why are there so many religions?" My answer is: because there exists one God who created, and continuously creates, a universe of wondrous diversity that can be rationally, if incompletely, understood. Part of this diversity includes the world's religious traditions. Lurking here are some epistemological assumptions I need to clarify.

First, as Paul Knittter has written, Christian experience of God as incarnated in the historical Jesus as the Christ of faith is one of the main pushes toward a pluralistic theology of religions. This "push comes from two essential characteristics of Christian experience of God: mysterious and trinitarian."[8] To this, I would also add a third push: historical consciousness and postmodern experience, which relativizes all knowledge claims.[9] Our knowledge of anything, including any possible knowledge persons can have of God—or the Dao or Emptying—is limited by the cultural and historical points of view we occupy at the moment we claim to know anything. Historical consciousness also teaches us that the reality of God, which Christians apprehend incarnated in the historical Jesus as the

7. Berthrong, *The Divine Deli*, 23.

8. Knitter, *Jesus and the Other Names*, 37.

9. See Harvey, *The Historian and the Believer*.

Christ of faith, is not limited by or confined to what Christians apprehend or believe. Accordingly, just as historical consciousness tells us that every glimpse of truth we have is intrinsically finite and conditioned, so "religious consciousness"—religious experience contextualized by the historicity of all knowledge—tells us that God is much more than any human being can imagine.

Accordingly, Hindu, Buddhist, Confucian–Daoist, Jewish, Muslim, or Christian religious experience—which must take place within the limits of historical and cultural contexts if they are to be experienced at all—has paradoxical edges. As a Lutheran Christian, I take this to mean that any particular experience of God is as mysterious as it is real, as ambiguous as it is reliable. Christian mystical and nonmystical theologians who have sensed and urged this recognition of God's utter mystery populate the history of Christian theological reflection: St. Paul, Augustine, Thomas Aquinas, Julian of Norwich, Margarite Porete, Meister Eckhart, Martin Luther, John Calvin, John Wesley, Paul Tillich, Karl Rahner, Edward Schillebeekx, Thoms Merton, and my teacher in process theology, John B. Cobb Jr., to cite just a few

Second, the paradox that sits at the heart of Christian faith, experience, and theological reflection is the Incarnation: in the life, death, and resurrection of a Jewish peasant two thousand years ago in a backwater region of the Roman Empire, human beings encountered God within the realities of historical existence. No question. Or appropriating the words of Luther's *Small Catechism*, "This is most certainly true." But while the historical Jesus reveals God, the Incarnation does not reveal all that God is—or is not. I suspect that most Christian talk about the Incarnation as "God in human form" or the "fullness of the divine mystery in the historical Jesus or the Christian Right's unqualified assertion that "Jesus is Lord" violates the meaning of the Incarnation more than preserving it. The Incarnation does not mean that the historical Jesus took on all that constitutes God or that God took on all that constitutes being human. So if the historical Jesus as the Christ of faith, as the second *persona* of the Trinity, defines *who* God is for Christians, the historical Jesus as the Christ of faith does not exhaust *what* God is. Ignoring the limitation of the incarnation is to fall into docetism—the heresy that so stresses the divinity of the historical Jesus that it denatures his humanity. Much fundamentalist and evangelical Christian theology is docetic.

Consequently, perceiving God's incarnation in the historical Jesus as the Christ of faith simultaneously recognizes that God cannot be limited to the historical Jesus. Or as Edward Schillebeekx writes:

> The revelation of God in Jesus, as the Christian gospel proclaims, does not mean that God absolutizes a historical particularity (be it even in Jesus of Nazareth). From that revelation in Jesus we learn that no single historical particularity can be called absolute and therefore, because of the relativity present in Jesus, every person can encounter God outside Jesus, especially in our worldly history and in the many religions that have arisen from it.[10]

No particular religious tradition, therefore, can have the final or exclusive or inclusive Word about God. Final words limit and demystify God and are more useful for the politics of power in Church hierarchies —or political hierarchies—than to the needs of faithful religious persons. Final words are, as Willfred Cantwell Smith liked to say, forms of idolatry—*shirk*, according to the Qur'an—that reduce God to that which is not God and surrendering to it.[11] An idol is not something that mediates God to human beings, but something that seeks to confine God to a set of theological propositions or a liturgical system or a particular book or a particular religions institution claimed to be the final mediator of God. Most idols occur in our individual and collective heads.

Third, if one reflects carefully about it, the reality holding things together that Christians name "God" cannot be confined to any one religious tradition because God—in the language of process theology, God's primordial nature and God's consequent nature—is both unity and plurality. That is, God is one and God is plural. God's "primordial nature," meaning God's self-identity as God through the moments of God's time, is what God always is as God, beyond the categories of thought and always in interdependent relationship with the universe God created and continues creating and sustaining. Yet the primordial nature of God is always in nondual interdependency with the "plurality" of God's consequent nature—God as God mutually affects and is affected by all things and events in the universe throughout the moments of God's experience.

My point is *not* that God has one nature interdependently expressed in different religious traditions, although this seems to me to be true. My point *is* that there are real and genuine differences within what medieval

10. Schillebeekx, *The Church: The Human Story of God*, 184.
11. W. C. Smith, *Belief and Faith*, chap. 3.

Christian mystical theology referred to as "the Godhead" and what process theology calls God's "primordial nature" and God's continual interaction with the universe and the plurality of human communities that constitute God's "consequent nature." As Alfred North Whitehead put it, since God cannot be an exception to the metaphysical principles through which God creates and sustains the universe, plurality seems essential to reality—"the way things really are"—from subatomic particles to religious traditions to God. Consequently, the historical Buddha was utterly correct: interdependence is at the heart of existence. Accordingly, Christians can trust that the plurality of the world's religions cannot be reduced to a kind of unity that would remove real differences among the various traditions to prove the superiority of one and the inferiority of the rest.

Lastly, the fact that similarities of teaching, practice, and ethical principles cut across the boundaries of specific religious traditions does not in itself constitute evidence for my theological interpretation of religious pluralism. There are also defining differences between the world's religious traditions, differences that express non-negotiationables that define the distinctive character of each tradition. For example, Christian experience and teaching regarding the Incarnation is not something Christians can compromise and still meaningfully participate in a distinctively Christian faith community. Likewise, Islamic monotheism is a call to not reduce God to that which cannot be God and surrender to it, which means that no Muslim can accept any form of the Christian doctrines of the Trinity or Incarnation and remain within the House of Islam. Similarly, Jewish monotheism leaves no room for the Christian doctrine of God's Incarnation in the historical Jesus as the Christ of faith. Buddhist nontheism is incommensurable with Jewish, Christian, and Islamic monotheism. Even as reading the *Bhagavad-Gīta* still clarifies Christian experience of the Incarnation for me, Christian affirmation of a single incarnation of God in a particular human life is incommensurable with the *Gīta*'s notion of many incarnations of Brahman in the myriad of deities of Hindu experience and teaching. What Buddhists mean by Awakening is not identical with what Christian tradition means by redemption.

But one need not assume that all religious doctrines and beliefs are commensurable. Clearly, they are not. Nor need one assume that similar experiences and ideas that cut across religious boundaries possess more evidentiary value than the non-negotiationables that separate particular religious traditions from one another. In this regard, three points can be made. First, incommensurable teachings and practices need not always imply contradiction. Often, differences between religious persons and communities are complementary. Christian experience of God as personal also includes experience of God as nonpersonal, as in, for example, Christian mystical experience. Likewise, Buddhist nontheism includes important elements of devotional experience quite similar to the structure of Christian devotional experience, as in the Jōdō Sninshū or the "True Pure Land School" founded by the Japanese monk Shinran Shōnin in the thirteenth century. While I am a Lutheran Christian who thinks that the Incarnation points to how God has always worked in the universe, and continues working, the Incarnation of God in the historical Jesus as the Christ of faith does not exhaust the reality of God, which means that the faith and practices of my non-Christian brothers and sisters can teach me lessons I need to understand.

Second, incommensurable teachings and practices running throughout the world's religious traditions, as well as incommensurable teachings and practices that are internal to every particular religious tradition, should surprise no one. The religious traditions of humanity are best understood as limited, historically and culturally contextualized apprehensions by which human beings have grasped and been grasped by what historians of religions of my generation often referred to as "the Sacred." According to most of humanity's religious traditions, as I have noted, the Reality that holds and underlies all things and events in the universe together is quite literally beyond capture by means of the categories of human language—which does not imply that linguistic constructions are not necessary or unimportant. So when it comes down to it, what I as an historian of religions name "the Sacred" and as a Lutheran theologian name "God incarnated in the life, death and resurrection of the historical Jesus as the Christ of faith," is ineffable Mystery. This Mystery can certainly be glimpsed and experienced contextually, but only partially and incompletely. But just because "the Sacred" as it is cannot be known completely or expressed in any final way does not mean that human beings cannot say and know *something* about the Sacred.

Finally, incommensurable teachings and practices may be and often are, radically contradictory, as exemplified by the differences between Christian, Jewish, Islamic monotheism and Buddhist nontheism. To Muslims surrendering to the call of the Qur'an not to reduce God to that which cannot be God, the Christian doctrines of Incarnation and the Trinity can only seem like "idolatry" (*shirk*). Christians who apprehend God incarnated in the life, death, and resurrection of the historical Jesus as the norm of faith and practice must be in disagreement with the Qur'an's portrayal of Jesus as an extraordinary prophet, but not a redeemer. In instances such as these, either conflicting doctrines are false—neither corresponds to reality—or one is true, or at least truer than its opposite. But how does one decide given that fact that religious persons faithful to their traditions can only relate to their religious traditions from within the perspective of their own traditions? Human beings seem unable to be religious "in general," but only "in particular."

In reflecting on this difficult issue, it helps to remember that the pluralist theology I affirm does not presuppose that all religious doctrine and practices equally correspond to the structure of reality, "the way things really are," or that all religious traditions are equally valid. It is very difficult to argue that White Supremacy is a truthful expression of Christianity or that terrorism carried out by Islamic radicals is an authentic expression of the Qur'an's call that human beings should "know each other." In these examples, distinguishing truth from falsehood is rather easy. But deciding whether Buddhist nontheism or Christian monotheism is a truer representation of Reality is quite another matter. So while I think that it is reasonable to argue that the world's religious traditions point to a common referent, it certainly is *not* reasonable to assert that these traditions are equally true or that one tradition is truer than the rest. No human being possesses enough knowledge to make either judgment. We may affirm, for example, that a particular tradition, doctrine, or practice is the best account of the Sacred *for us*; we cannot do so for anyone else, as H. Richard Niebuhr used to argue.[12] Theological reflection is always confessional. Which means that interreligious dialogue in a world of religious pluralism is an absolute necessity so that one's confessional standpoint can be stretched and deepened.

A further point requires clarification. As I have noted, the natural sciences need to be brought into the practice of interreligious dialogues as a contributing partner since in this postmodern age, all religious persons must understand and practice their faith in the context of what the natural sciences are revealing about the amazing physical structures of the universe.[13] What the sciences are revealing about the physical structures

---

12. See Niebuhr, *The Meaning of Revelation*.

13. For an extended argument on this point see Ingram, *Buddhist–Christian Dialogue in an Age of Science*, chap. 1.

of nature both challenge, and, if approached with care, deepen religious faith and practice wherever it is found. According to Whiteheadian process theology, God is immanent within the physical processes of nature. When taken together with the extraordinary explanatory power of the natural sciences, the most coherent conclusion must be that "the Sacred," however it is "named," is "in, with, and under" the universe's unfolding natural processes of which "the Sacred" is the transcendent reality beyond name and form, holding all name and form together in a wondrous unity that embodies an incredible pluralism. Some of this pluralism is constituted by the religious traditions of humanity.

But given everything I have written in this book, the question now is, "So what?" Every theological reflection, every theologian to whom I have listened or read invariably crashes, sometimes headlong, into this question. This is so because not only was the historical Jesus not interested in "religion," I can't remember reading any mainline Christian theologian who claims that God is interested in "religion" either. In fact, if one believes the New Testament—and the Tanak, the Qur'an, the Vedas, the Buddhist Canon, or the *Dao De Ching*—God has never been interested in an abstraction called "religion." So it seems that the one and only test of a valid religious idea or experience is pragmatic, or as Jesus is reported to have said, "You know them by their works." A valid religious idea, doctrine, practice, or religious experience leads directly to practical compassion and love. "Compassion" is knowing by experience the utter interdependence of all things caught up in the field of space-time, so that the suffering of any living being is one's own suffering, just as the joy of any living being is also, partly, one's own. Compassion engenders love, meaning active social engagement with the world in nonviolent (if possible) struggle against systemic social, economic, and political structures of injustice that cause suffering to human beings and the creatures of nature.

Accordingly, if one's understanding of God makes one kinder, more empathetic, more impelled to act justly through concrete nonviolent acts of loving-kindness—at least as far possible in a universe in which life must eat life to survive—one should take this as a sign that one has a truthful understanding of God. I think this is true whether one is a Christian, Jew, Muslim, Hindu, Buddhist, follower of the Dao, or an avowed "secularist." But if one's notion of God has made one unkind, brittle of spirit, belligerent, cruel, or self-righteous, or has led one to kill in God's name, one has an untruthful understanding of God. I also think this is true whether one is a Christian, Jew, Muslim, Hindu, Buddhist, follower of the Dao, or an avowed "secularist." As Wilfred Cantwell Smith wisely wrote, there is no such thing as "religion" because "religion" as a noun is an abstraction from the experiences of what actual religious persons do. "Religion" is more like a verb or an adjective pointing to what real human beings do to link themselves to, or be linked by, the Sacred experienced and named differently in the plurality of humanity's religious traditions—a reality, as the Buddhists say, that is beyond "name and form," or as Sufi and Christian mystics say, is beyond all words or theological labels.

This is why I think Thomas Merton wrote that religious practice should be about "entering the silence" because that's where we find God— or as a Lutheran would put it, where God finds us—and then like Mahatma Gandhi or Martin Luther King reenter the world and struggle to overcome the injustice of oppressive systems of political, economic, racial, and gender injustice. My suspicion is that the Sacred Reality I name "God" is found everywhere, including the noise of our lives, and Merton would have probably not denied this. But human beings experience God most often in silence—Jesus in the silence of the desert for forty days, the Buddha sitting in meditation for forty-nine days (although he didn't name what he found in the silence "God"), Moses alone on Mt. Sinai, Mohammed sitting in a dessert cave, Daoist sages alone in nature. I am certainly not an accomplished mystic like Merton, Jesus, the Buddha, Moses, Mohammad, the Daoist sages, or my favorite medieval Christian mystic, Margarite Porete. But like these mystics, I have come to think that the silence is all there really is. It is the Alpha and Omega. It is God brooding over the face of the deep, the blended notes of ten thousand things, the whine of wings, the music of Bach and Mozart, the physics of Einstein and Bohr. We take a step in the right direction to pray to this silence. Here all distinctions blur and we quit our tents and pray without ceasing.

# Bibliography

Akhilananda, Swami. *Hindu Psychology: Its Meaning for the West*. New York: Harper, 1946.

Ali, A. Yusuf, trans. *The Holy Qur'an: English Translation of the Meanings and Commentary*. King Fahd Complex for he Printing of the Holy Qur'an, 2002.

Bainton, Roland. *Here I Stand: A Life of Martin Luther*. Nashville: Abingdon, 1950.

Barbour, Ian G. *Religion and Science: Historical and Contemporary Issues*. San Francisco: HaperSanFrancisco, 2000.

Berger, Peter L. *The Heretical Imperative: Contemporary Possibilities of Religious Affirmation*. Garden City, NY: Doubeday, 1979.

Borg, Marcus J. *Jesus: Uncovering the Life, Teachings, and Relevance of a Revolutionary*. New York: HarperCollins, 2006.

Bornkamm, Günther. *Paul*. Translated by D. M. G. Stalker. New York: Harper & Row, 1971.

Brockington, J. L. *The Sacred Thread: A Short History of Hinduism*. 2nd ed. Oxford: Oxford University Press, 2000.

Buford, Grace C. "If the Buddha Is So Great, Why Are These People Christians?" In *Buddhists Talk about Jesus, Christians Talk about the Buddha*, edited by Rita M. Gross and Terry C. Muck, 131–37. New York: Continuum, 2000.

Bultmann, Rudolf. *Theology of the New Testament*. Vol. 2. Translated by Kendrick Grobel. New York: Scribner, 1955.

Chan, Wing-tsit. *A Source Book in Chinese Philosophy*. Princeton: Princeton University Press, 1963.

Ching, Julia. *Chinese Religions*. Maryknoll, NY: Orbis, 1993.

———. "East Asian Religions." In *World Religions: Eastern Traditions*, edited by Willard G. Oxtoby. Oxford: Oxford University Press, 1996.

Christenson, Tom. "The Oddest Word: Paradoxes of Theological Discourse." In *The Boundaries of Knowledge in Buddhism, Christianity, and Science*, edited by Paul D. Numrich, 164–83. Religion, Theology, and Natural Science 15. Göttingen: Vandenhoeck & Ruprecht, 2008.

Cleary, Thomas, trans. *The Art of War: Sun Tzu*. Boston: Shambala, 1988.

Cobb, John B., Jr. *Beyond Dialogue: Toward a Mutual Transformation of Christianity and Buddhism*. 1982. Reprinted, Eugene, OR: Wipf & Stock, 1998.

———. "Can a Christian Be a Buddhist, Too?" *Japanese Religions* 10 (December 1978) 1–20.

———. "Contacts with Buddhism: A Christian Confession." In *Beside Still Waters: Jews, Christians, and the Way of the Buddha*, edited by Harold Kasimow, John P. Keenan, and Linda Klepinger Keenan, 115–28. Boston: Wisdom, 2003.

———. "Theological Response." In *The Dialogue Comes of Age: Christian Encounters With Other Traditions*, edited by John B. Cobb Jr., and Ward M. McAfee, 185–211. Minneapolis: Fortress, 2010.

# Bibliography

Cohn-Sherbok, Dan. *Judaism: History, Belief, and Practice*. London: Routledge, 2003.

Cragg, Kenneth, and R. Marston Speight. *The House of Islam*. 3rd ed. New York: Wadsworth, 1988.

Dallal, Ahmad. "Science, Medicine, and Technology." In *The Oxford History of Islam*, edited by John L. Esposito, 155–214. Oxford: Oxford University Press, 1999.

Dawkins, Richard. *The Blind Watchmaker*. New York: Norton, 1986.

De Bary, William, ed. *Sources of Chinese Tradition*. 2 vols. 2nd ed. New York: Columbia University Press, 1999.

Dunne, John S. *The Way of All The Earth: Experiments in Truth and Religion*. Notre Dame: University of Notre Dame Press, 1978.

Dyson, Freeman J. *Origins of Life*. Cambridge: Cambridge University Press, 1985.

Eck, Diana L. *A New Religious America: How a "Christian Country" Has Now Become the World's Most Religiously Diverse Nation*. San Francisco: HarperSanFrancisco, 2001.

Efron, John, Steven Weitzman, Matthias Lehman, and Joshua Holo. *The Jews: A History*. Upper Saddle River, NJ: Pearson Prentice Hall, 2009.

Eisley, Loren. "The Hidden Teacher." In *The Unexpected Universe*, 48–66. New York: Harcourt, 1969.

Esposito, John. *Islam: The Straight Path*. Oxford: Oxford University Press, 2004.

———. *What Everyone Needs to Know about Islam*. 2nd ed. Oxford: Oxford University Press, 2011.

Fleischner, Eva. "Jews and Christians through the Ages." In *The Dialogue Comes of Age: Christian Encounters with Other Traditions*, edited by John B. Cobb Jr. and Ward M. McAfee, 41–85. Minneapolis: Fortress, 2010.

Flood, Gavin. *An Introduction to Hinduism*. Cambridge: Cambridge University Press, 1996.

Habito, Maria Reis. "On Becoming a Buddhist Christian." In *Beside Still Waters: Jews, Christians, and the Way of the Buddha*, edited by Harold Kasimow, John P. Keenan, and Linda Klepinger Keenan, 301–13. Boston: Wisdom Publications, 2003.

Habito, Ruben L. F. *Experiencing Buddhism: Ways of Wisdom and Compassion*. Maryknoll, NY: Orbis, 2005.

Haemig, Mary Jane. "Luther on Translating the Bible." *Word & Word* 21 (2011) 255–62.

Harvey, Van A. *The Historian and the Believer*. Philadelphia: Westminster, 1966.

Hawking, Stephen. *A Brief History of Time*. New York: Bantam, 2005.

Hick, John. *God Has Many Names*. Philadelphia: Westminster, 1982.

———. *An Interpretation of Religion: Human Responses to the Transcendent*. New Haven: Yale University Press, 1989.

Hilberg, Raul. *The Destruction of the European Jews*. New Haven: Yale University Press, 2003.

Hussain, Amir. *Oil and Water: Two Faiths, One God*. Kelowna, BC: CopperHouse, 2006.

Ingram, Paul O. *The Dharma of Faith: An Introduction to Classical Pure Land Buddhism*. Washington, DC: University Press of America, 1977.

———. "Avoiding Fundamentalism and Relativism: A Pluralist Lutheran Theology." *Dialog: A Journal of Theology* 15 (2012) 330–37.

———. *The Modern Buddhist–Christian Dialogue Two Universalistic Religions in Transformation*. Studies in Comparative Religion 2. Lewiston, NY: Mellen, 1988.

———. "On the Practice of Faith: A Lutheran's Interior Dialogue with Buddhism." *Buddhist–Christian Studies* 21 (2001) 43–50.

———. *The Process of Buddhist–Christian Dialogue*. Eugene, OR: Cascade Books, 2009.

————. "Shinran Shōnin and Martin Luther: A Soteriological Comparison. *Journal of the American Academy of Religion* 31 (1971) 430–47.

————. *Theological Reflections at the Boundaries.* Eugene, OR: Cascade Books, 2012.

————. *Wrestling with the Ox: A Theology of Religious Experience.* 1997. Reprinted, Eugene, OR: Wipf & Stock, 2006.

Johnston, William. *Christian Zen: A Way of Meditation.* 2nd ed. San Francisco: Harper & Row, 1979.

Jonas, Robert A. "Loving Someone You Can't See." In *Beside Still Waters: Jews, Christians, and the Way of the Buddha,* edited by Harold Kasimow, John P. Keenan, and Linda Klepinger Keenan, 143–57. Boston: Wisdon, 2003.

Kittelson, James M. *Luther the Reformer.* Minneapolis: Fortress, 2003.

Knitter, Paul F. *Jesus and the Other Names: Christian Mission and Global Responsibility.* Maryknoll, NY: Orbis, 1996.

————. *Without Buddha, I Could not Be a Christian.* Oxford: One World, 2009.

Kolb, Robert, and Timothy J. Wengert, eds. *The Book of Concord: The Confessions of the Evangelical Lutheran Church.* Minneapolis: Fortress, 2000.

Lakotos, Imre, and Alan Musgrave, eds. *Criticism and the Growth of Knowledge.* Studies in Logic and the Foundations of Mathematics. Proceedings 4. Cambridge: Cambridge University Press, 1970.

Lew, Alan, "Becoming Who You Always Were: The Story of a Zen Rabbi." In *Beside Still Waters: Jews, Christians, and the Way of the Buddha,* edited by Harold Kasimow, John P. Keenan, and Linda Klepinger Keenan, 45–60. Boston: Wisdon Publications, 2003.

Lopez, Donald, ed. *Religions of China in Practice.* Princeton: Princeton University Press, 1999.

Lubarsky, Sandra B. "Enriching Awareness: A Jewish Encounter with Buddhism." In *Beside Still Waters: Jew, Christians, and the Way of the Buddha,* edited by Harold Kasimow, John P. Keenan, and Linda Klippinger Keenan, 61–70. Boston: Wisdom Publications, 2003.

Matsunaga, Daigan, and Alicia Matsunaga. *Foundation of Japanese Buddhism.* 2 vols. Los Angeles: Buddhist Books International, 1974–76.

Melton, J. Gordon, and Martin Baumann, eds. *Religions of the World: A Comprehensive Encyclopedia of Beliefs and Practices.* 2nd ed. ABC-CLEO eBooks, 2010.

Merton, Thomas. *Mystics & Zen Masters.* A Delta Book. New York: Dell, 1967.

Murata, Sachiko, and William C. Chittick. *The Vision of Islam.* St. Paul, MN: Paragon House, 1994.

Nhat Hanh, Thich. *Being Peace.* Edited by Arnold Kotler. Berkeley: Parallex, 1987.

Niebuhr, H. Richard. *The Meaning of Revelation.* Philadelphia: Westminster, 2006.

Rad, Gerhard von. *Old Testament Theology.* Vol. 1, *The Theology of Israel's Historical Traditions.* Translated by D. M. G. Stalker. New York: Harper & Row, .

Radhakrishnan, Servepalli, and Charles A. Moore, eds. *A Sourcebook in Indian Philosophy.* Princeton: Princeton University Press, 1957.

Ridderbos, Herman N. *Paul: An Outline of His Theology.* Translated by Richard de Witt. Grand Rapids: Eerdmans, 1975.

Rosenberg, Roy A. *The Concise Guide to Judaism: History, Practice, Faith.* Denver: Mentor Books, 1991.

Ruether, Rosemary Radford. *Faith and Fratricide: The Theological Roots of Anti-Semitism.* 1979. Reprinted, Eugene, OR: Wipf & Stock, 1998.

Sachar, Howard M. *The Course of Modern Jewish History.* New York: Dell, 1977.

Schillebeeckx, Edward. *The Church: The Human Story of God*. Translated by John Bowden. New York: Crossroad, 1990.

Schimmel, Annemarie. *Mystical Dimensions of Islam*. Chapel Hill: University of North Carolina Press, 1975.

Scholem, Gershom. *Major Trends in Jewish Mysticism*. New York: Schocken, 1954.

Schumann, H. W. *The Historical Buddha: The Times, Life, and Teachings of the Founder*. Translated by M. O. C. Walshe. London: Arkana, 1989.

Sells, Michael. The *Mystical Languages of Unsaying*. Chicago: University of Chicago Press, 1994.

Seltzer, Robert M. *Judaism: A People and Its History, Religion, History, and Culture*. New York: Macmillan, 1989.

Smith, Barbara Herrnstein. *Belief and Resistance: Dynamics of Contemporary Intellectual Controversy*. Cambridge: Harvard University Press, 1997.

———. *Scandalous Knowledge: Science, Truth, and the Human*. Frontiers of Theory. Edinburgh: Edinburgh University Press, 2005.

Smith, Wilfred Cantwell. *Faith and Belief*. Princeton: Princeton University Press, 1979.

———. *Islam in Modern History*. Princeton: Princeton University Press, 1957.

Spitz, Lewis W., Sr., trans. *Preface to the Complete Edition of Luther's Latin Writings* (1545) in *Luther's Works*, vol. 36. Edited by Theodore Bachman. Philadelphia: Muhlenberg, 1960.

———. *Scandalous Knowledge: Science, Truth, and the Human*. Durham: Duke University Press, 2006.

Suzuki, Shinryu. *Zen Mind, Beginner's Mind*. New York: Weatherhill, 1979.

Thompson, Laurence G. *Chinese Religion: An Introduction*. 5th ed. Belmont, CA: Wadsworth, 1996.

Thurston, Bonnie. "'The Buddha Offered Me a Raft.'" In *Buddhists Talk about Jesus, Christians Talk about the Buddha*, edited by Rita M. Gross and Terry C. Muck, 118–30. New York: Continuum, 2000.

Unno, Mark. "Compartive Theology with A Difference: A Shin Buddhist View in Pedagogical Perspective." In *Criteria of Discernment in Interreligious Dialogue*, edited by Catherine Cornille, 255–77. Interreligious Dialogue Series 1. Eugene, OR: Cascade Books, 2009.

Waley, Arthur, trans. *The Analects of Confucius*. New York: Vintage, 1938.

———. *The Way And Its Power: A Study of the Tao Te Ching and Its Place in Chinese Thought*. New York: Grove, 1958.

Welch, Holmes. *Taoism: The Parting of the Way*. Rev. ed. New York: Beacon, 1965.

Wilhelm, Hellmut. *Eight Lectures on the I Ching*. Translated by Cary F. Baynes. New York: Harper & Row, 1960.

Whitehead, Alfred North. *Process and Reality: An Essay in Cosmology*. Corrected ed. Edited by David Ray Griffin and Donald W. Sherburne. Gifford Lectures 1927/28. New York: Free Press, 1985.

Yang, C. K. *Religion in Chinese Society: A Study of Contemporary Social Functions of Religion and Some of Their Historical Factors*. Berkeley: University of California, 1961.

Yu-lan, Fung. *A Sort History of Chinese Philosophy*. Edited by Derk Bodde. New York: Macmillan, 1964.

# Index of Names

# Scripture Index

~